THE 100 BEST BIRDWATCHING SITES IN AUSTRALIA

THE 100 BEST BIRDWATCHING SITES IN AUSTRALIA

SUE TAYLOR

JOHN BEAUFOY PUBLISHING

Contents

Ken Haines

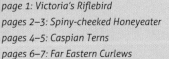

page 1: Victoria's Riflebird
pages 2–3: Spiny-cheeked Honeyeater
pages 4–5: Caspian Terns
pages 6–7: Far Eastern Curlews

Jim Smart

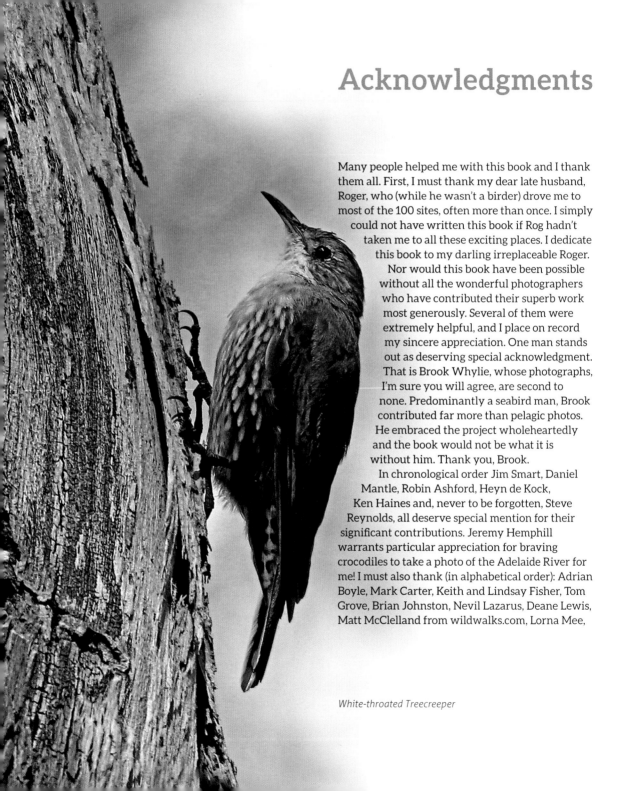

Acknowledgments

Many people helped me with this book and I thank them all. First, I must thank my dear late husband, Roger, who (while he wasn't a birder) drove me to most of the 100 sites, often more than once. I simply could not have written this book if Rog hadn't taken me to all these exciting places. I dedicate this book to my darling irreplaceable Roger. Nor would this book have been possible without all the wonderful photographers who have contributed their superb work most generously. Several of them were extremely helpful, and I place on record my sincere appreciation. One man stands out as deserving special acknowledgment. That is Brook Whylie, whose photographs, I'm sure you will agree, are second to none. Predominantly a seabird man, Brook contributed far more than pelagic photos. He embraced the project wholeheartedly and the book would not be what it is without him. Thank you, Brook.

In chronological order Jim Smart, Daniel Mantle, Robin Ashford, Heyn de Kock, Ken Haines and, never to be forgotten, Steve Reynolds, all deserve special mention for their significant contributions. Jeremy Hemphill warrants particular appreciation for braving crocodiles to take a photo of the Adelaide River for me! I must also thank (in alphabetical order): Adrian Boyle, Mark Carter, Keith and Lindsay Fisher, Tom Grove, Brian Johnston, Nevil Lazarus, Deane Lewis, Matt McClelland from wildwalks.com, Lorna Mee,

White-throated Treecreeper

Danielle Mobbs from Sacred Earth Safaris, Helen Monro, Parks Victoria, Ed Pierce, Steve Potter, Di Quick, Mick Roderick, Danielle Schroder, Jack Shick Photography, Lord Howe Island, Liz Stinson, Tom Tarrant, Helen Toop, Peter Waanders and Roger Williams.

I said Rog drove me to most of the sites in this book. Other sites I visited with professional guides and I thank them all. Klaus Uhlenhut from Kirrama Wildlife Tours took me to Cape York, Fogg Dam, Parry Lagoons, Hasties Swamp, Buffalo Creek, Mission Beach, Iron Range, Rinyirru (Lakefield) National Park, Kakadu, Kununurra, Adelaide River Crossing, Knuckey Lagoon, Katherine and the Mitchell Plateau. Phil Maher from Australian Ornithological Services Pty Ltd (famous for Plains-wanderer tours) took me to Lake Gilles Conservation Park and Dhilba Guuranda-Innes National Park. I visited both these spots again with Peter Waanders of Bellbird Birding Tours and also went up the Birdsville Track with him. This included Gluepot Reserve and the Flinders Ranges. Steve Davidson, The Melbourne Birder, showed me my first Sooty Owl. Rohan Clarke arranges pelagics out of Eaglehawk Neck in Tasmania and is very generous with his ornithological expertise. Neil Macumber from Birdswing Birding and Wildlife Tours arranges Port Fairy pelagics (and his partner, Alison Bainbridge, provides delicious morning teas). I went to Macquarie Island with Heritage Expeditions and to the Abrolhos with Coates Wildlife Tours. I visited Christmas and Cocos Islands four times with Richard Baxter (who has since proved a wonderful source of birdy information). The Daintree River Cruise I did twice with Chris Dahlberg. It is now run by Murray Hunt. I visited Green Cape with the late great Graham Pizzey. Lloyd Nielsen's birding directories alerted me to Wonga Wetlands, Mogareeka Inlet and Comerong Island Nature Reserve. Details of his guides are in the bibliography. I acknowledge the traditional custodians of the land and water of all these special sites.

I should thank the experts I've never met, who answered my questions kindly. David Milton from CSIRO explained the breeding sites for Bar-tailed Godwits, Cheryl Gole from BirdLife Australia provided information about Important Bird Areas, Steve Anyon-Smith talked to me about the birds of Royal National Park. Bob Semmens updated me about Mallacoota after the devastating bushfires of 2019.

Supportive friends should never be overlooked. Helen and Dugald Monro, Helen Toop and my cousin Liz Hooper all come into this category. I must also thank Rae Clark, a never-ending source of birdy knowledge.

My heartfelt thanks go to you all. I hope you enjoy the result.

Introduction

It has been an absolute joy writing this book. What a wonderful excuse to go back through all my field notes and photographs, and to relive all the fun I had birding at all sorts of exciting places.

So often I find myself writing about threatened and endangered species, worrying about the menace of foxes and feral cats. So much development occurs without due consideration of the long-term effects on the environment. I chide civilisation for its self-centred mismanagement of the countryside on a scale that only mankind could achieve. Then I rejoice when some land is protected in a national park, believing it should now be a permanent haven for native species. But often I'm forced to repudiate my celebrations when governments betray their responsibilities and allow inappropriate activities in our parks. If we do not preserve appropriate habitat, our native species will not survive. It's as simple as that. And who will be to blame? Each and every one of us who did not speak out.

So what a pleasure to put my cruasading behind me, and, on this occasion, to concentrate on our beautiful birds and the best places to see them. Because, the best efforts of politicians notwithstanding, we still do have many special places to go birding, and here you will find my best 100 sites.

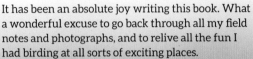

Eastern Yellow Robin

Jim Smart

My first decision was how to select my top 100 sites. What is a site, anyway? Is a national park a site? Or must it be more geographically discrete? Can it only be, say, a maximum of a square kilometre? Can the Birdsville Track be a site? In anyone's language, it is a trifle cheeky to categorise a road that is over 500 kilometres long, as a 'site'. At the very least, it is a collection of several sites. However, each of these on its own would not be worthy of inclusion in this volume. Taken together, they certainly warrant attention. So my definition of a site is relatively flexible. Sometimes it is quite specific (such as Hasties Swamp); sometimes it is huge (Rinyirru [Lakefield] National Park); sometimes it is lengthy (the Strzelecki Track); sometimes it is a district or an area (Katherine or Chiltern). A site is somewhere I've travelled to in order to go birding, and have enjoyed myself seeing either a large number of species or a large number of special birds.

I started off thinking I wouldn't include any sites that didn't have 100 species of birds. Very quickly I realised that that wouldn't work. Macquarie Island, site number 4 on my list, has only a handful of species, but boy has it got a lot of birds! It simply had to be included. In fact, several of the island sites don't have 100 species on their lists, but they provide great birding. This is simply my list of sites where I've had most fun birding. It is absolutely, unapologetically subjective.

It was hard leaving out some of my favourite places. It was difficult not including Shipwreck Creek, near Mallacoota, where we go looking for Eastern Ground Parrots, Southern Emu-wrens and Tawny-crowned Honeyeaters – three special birds. But there isn't much else there, and I didn't think that three special birds were enough.

I made no attempt to cover every Australian bird species. Let's be honest, it's not a lot of fun trudging through hot prickly triodia looking for Carpentarian Grasswrens. This book is about having fun birding. If you visit every one of these 100 sites, you will not see every Australian bird. I cannot guarantee that you'll see a Savanna Nightjar on Christmas Island or a Long-tailed Cuckoo on Norfolk, but I believe I can say without fear of contradiction, that you'll have wonderful birding at each and every one of my best 100 birding sites.

I've made very few changes for the third edition. There has been no reason to add or delete sites, and, luckily, there have been few bird name changes since the second edition. I'm using nomenclature of IOC 12.2. I have updated species' conservation status and population estimates. Sadly, both Swift Parrots and Plains-wanderers have been reclassified as critically endangered but happily, Southern Cassowaries have been reclassified from vulnerable to least concern.

So please enjoy my personal 100 best birdwatching sites. As you do so, delight in our glorious birds, and thrill at our wonderful, unique countryside. If you get half the enjoyment visiting these sites that I have, you will be extremely well rewarded.

Bar-tailed Godwits fly to Broome from Siberia. These newly arrived birds are still sporting some of their breeding plumage.

1

Broome

Put simply, Broome is a tropical paradise. Located on the Kimberley coast in far north-west Western Australia, Broome is exquisitely remote. Eighty Mile Beach (which is actually 140 miles or 220 kilometres long), between Broome and Port Hedland, is the most important area for waders in Australia. South and east of Broome on the Indian Ocean, Roebuck Bay must be close behind. This is where the Broome Bird Observatory has been established, half an hour's drive from the township of Broome.

The first time I visited Broome was in 1982, when my late husband, Roger, and I drove from Perth to Darwin and enjoyed a couple of nights in Broome along the way. Broome is about halfway, being 2,200 kilometres north of Perth and 2,000 kilometres from Darwin. We admired Black Kites with their distinctive forked tails, gorgeous Red-winged Parrots and, of course, lots of waders.

When we returned ten years later, I photographed Tawny Frogmouths at the observatory and a Barking Owl in the town roosting above a nest of White-gaped Honeyeaters, which he watched assiduously until the chicks were large enough to make a meal. Rather stupidly, we found ourselves up to our thighs in mud up Little Crab Creek looking for Mangrove Golden Whistlers. We saw Oriental Pratincoles, Dusky Gerygones, Red-headed Myzomelas, Canary White-eyes and spectacular White-breasted Whistlers.

In September 2009, I attended the Broome

Canary White-eyes are common at Broome, and very cute.

Black Kite
Singing Honeyeater
Rainbow Bee-eater
AND A SPECIAL ONE TO FIND
Mangrove Golden Whistler

Bird Observatory to do a course on 'The Birds of Broome'. It is no secret that I need all the help I can get identifying the birds of Broome, but the real purpose of this trip was to try to see a Common Redshank and a Broad-billed Sandpiper. I ticked the sandpiper quickly – I found it myself, on the first day, on the beach right at the observatory, easily identified with the snipe-like markings on its head, but I dipped on the redshank. The warden told me that there were four Common Redshanks residing in Roebuck Bay at the time, among 100,000 other waders. I don't know if this comment was designed to make me feel better, but it didn't.

Great Bowerbirds were common around the observatory and agile wallabies came in to drink at the bird bath, along with Broad-

Broome is possibly the easiest place to see the Broad-billed Sandpiper.

billed Flycatchers and Long-tailed Finches. We saw Brolgas, Yellow Chats, Red-backed Fairywrens and nail-tailed wallabies.

The warden put on a demonstration of mist netting and, after he'd banded, weighed and measured the birds, I was allowed to release some of them. What a privilege to hold Double-barred Finches and Rufous-throated Honeyeaters in my hands! The Peaceful Doves were put carefully on the ground, as they tend to shed feathers when held.

When I think of Broome today, I think of breathtaking flocks of waders wheeling around Roebuck Bay. I also think of majestic ghost gums, red earth, pindan scrub and the overwhelming heat. And beautiful Broad-billed Sandpipers.

Perhaps Australia's least active waterfowl, the Freckled Duck is nevertheless always exciting to see.

Sue Taylor

Orange-bellied Parrots were never a guaranteed sighting at Werribee, but today they are exceedingly rare.

Werribee sewage farm

2

Without a doubt, Victoria's best birding spot is the Werribee sewage farm, officially known as Melbourne Water's Western Treatment Plant. We Melbirdians are so lucky to have this inspirational destination right on our doorstep.

The farm is 35 kilometres from Melbourne along the Geelong Road and it takes just an hour to get there from the city. Interstate birders can fly into Avalon, hire a car, spend the day in the farm (which is tantamount to adjacent to the airport) and fly home that evening. Perfect. The only drawback is that they must have a key. Or know a friendly Melbirdian.

Birders come from all over the world to see breathtaking numbers of waterbirds at Werribee. There are a phenomenal 270 species on the Werribee bird list, including nine species of tern and 14 species of duck. The best time to visit is summer, when countless northern hemisphere waders are present and thousands of Australian Shelducks congregate to moult. You can rely on Sharp-tailed and Curlew Sandpipers, and Red-necked Stints, and often something rare turns up. One lost Stilt Sandpiper caused great excitement in 2011, as did a Tufted Duck in 2019. In 2020 an aberrant shelduck caused much debate and many twitchers tried very hard to convince themselves that it was actually a South African Shelduck, which (let's be fair) was pretty unlikely. Sadly, it seems it was a Paradise/Mountain Shelduck cross, escaped from a breeder.

In winter you'll see Double-banded Plovers on holiday from New Zealand. Winter used to be popular for Orange-bellied Parrots, but you'd be lucky to see one today. The total wild population is now estimated to be somewhere around 25 birds. They breed in Melaleuca in southern Tasmania in summer and spend the winter on the south coast of the mainland. My last sighting of wild Orange-bellied Parrots at Werribee was of six birds in 2007. I doubt I'll ever see one again. In 2019 I saw some birds that had been bred in captivity and released at Werribee, in the hope that they'll learn to migrate across Bass Strait. They were wearing lots of jewellery, just like the bird in the photo.

We always start our day at Werribee with a drive along Point Wilson Road to the Murtcaim Wildlife Area looking for Brolga. On the way we'll check out the Spit Nature Conservation Reserve and the T-Section Lagoons. No one visits Werribee for passerines, but there are Zebra Finches, Golden-headed Cisticolas, Striated Fieldwren and Little Grassbirds.

We visit the boat ramp, checking for seabirds, then we inspect Freckled Duck Rock, to see what ducks are loafing there. As the name suggests, Freckled Ducks used to be seen here reliably. We drive along the coast road, scanning every pond and beach. There'll be Cape Barren Geese, egrets, pelicans, cormorants, oystercatchers, Red-necked Avocets, Pied Stilts (formerly called White-headed Stilts and before that Black-winged Stilts) and other waders.

Better birders than I am clock up 100 species in a day at Werribee. I'm usually satisfied with my modest 80 or so. While it is possible to miss out on a particular species you might want, it is impossible to have a bad day birding at Werribee.

Pink-eared Duck
Red-necked Avocet
Red-necked Stint
Striated Fieldwren

One Australian White Ibis joins a flock of his Straw-necked cousins as they fly over a lagoon at Werribee, ignoring the You Yangs in the background.

Cairns

3

Several years ago, I was naive enough to believe some propaganda about proposed alterations to the Cairns Esplanade and the deleterious effect they were going to have on the birdlife. I wrote to the mayor of Cairns registering my objection. I received a polite reply, inviting me to come and make up my own mind when works were complete.

I was last in Cairns in 2022 (ticking the Nordmann's Greenshank) and I'm delighted to report that improvements to the Esplanade have been just that: improvements. Now the holidaying hordes congregate at the southern end, leaving the rest of the boardwalk for joggers and birders. Wonderful.

Whenever I'm in Cairns, I try to start the day with a walk along the Esplanade. It's famous for allowing birders to get close to waders. I've seen some great birds from that boardwalk. Black-necked Storks and Beach Stone-curlews leap to mind, as well as the aforementioned Nordmann's Greenshank. Naturally

When they feed quietly in the canopy, Double-eyed Fig Parrots are easily overlooked.

there are more waders over the summer months, but it's always good.

On the land side of the boardwalk, perhaps the best bird I've seen was a Double-eyed Fig Parrot. He was a gorgeous bright green little jewel with pretty facial markings and shiny black eyes. He sat still, obligingly at eye level, allowing me to admire him at my leisure.

Varied Honeyeaters are common and I've seen Sacred, Torresian and Forest Kingfishers here, although I have to go to the Botanic Gardens to tick

Heyn de Kock

Little Kingfishers. The Peaceful Doves are smaller than the ones I'm used to down south, but they're just as peaceful. In the early morning, Torresian Imperial Pigeons fly in to feed on the mainland during the day and return to their island homes in the late afternoon. If you venture into the mangroves to the north of the boardwalk, you may well be rewarded with a Mangrove Robin, but be sure to wear a good covering of insect repellent. I once had a violent reaction to bites received in those mangroves and had to wear long sleeves for a fortnight.

Once in Cairns, a Buff-banded Rail greeted me on the footpath outside our hotel in the main street. Olive-backed Sunbirds are common, but nonetheless beautiful, as are the Metallic Starlings.

On the way to the airport there are two mangrove boardwalks, which look very promising. My advice is: don't bother with them. They were poorly maintained last

time I visited, and the only birds I've ever seen there are Brown Honeyeaters and Spangled Drongos.

Instead, I would recommend the rainforest boardwalk at Centenary Lakes in the Botanic Gardens. Here you can see Orange-footed Scrubfowl, Green Orioles, Black Butcherbirds, Spectacled Monarchs, and, if you are lucky, Red-necked Crakes. You can also see Shining Flycatchers and Hornbill Friarbirds, as well as the sweet Little Kingfisher. If that's not enough, there are usually Bush Stone-curlews in the cemetery.

There are other places to visit around Cairns (such as Mount Whitfield Conservation Park) but, in my opinion, the Esplanade alone justifies Cairns a position in Australia's top ten birding sites.

Cairns Esplanade is a wonderful spot to view waders. Here we see Sharp-tailed Sandpipers, Greater and Lesser Sand Plovers, Red-necked Stints, Broad-billed Sandpipers and a Great Knot.

Heyn de Kock

Colourful Olive-backed Sunbirds are very common around Cairns.

Bush Stone-curlew
Far Eastern Curlew
Varied Honeyeater
AND ONE TO LOOK OUT FOR
Little Kingfisher

King and Royal Penguins parade past a sleeping weaner seal.

4

Macquarie Island

Macquarie Island is just a dot in the ocean, halfway between Australia and Antarctica. It rains every day and it's always windy and often misty. The sand is black, as it's derived from dark basaltic rocks. There are no trees, just grasses and megaherbs.

An island without trees doesn't sound very attractive. But believe me it's a very special place. I found it delightful and exhilarating. The penguins were captivating. Hundreds of thousands of them, some going about their business and ignoring me totally, some wanting to make friends. It was an unforgettable experience, truly the trip of a lifetime.

I visited Macquarie Island in December 2009 with Heritage Expeditions on the *Spirit of Enderby*. I went alone because Roger couldn't get travel insurance (due to his dicky heart). I say alone, but in fact I was accompanied by 42 other passengers, 13 staff and 22 Russian crew.

The island comprises some 130 square kilometres, 34 kilometres long and up to five kilometres wide. It is located 1,200 kilometres south of New Zealand, 1,500 kilometres south-south-east of Tasmania. It took us five days to get there from New Zealand. It is administered by the Tasmanian Parks and Wildlife Service, and accommodates a permanent base of the Australian National Antarctic Research Expeditions.

Everyone falls in love with the penguins. They really are most endearing. There are 800,000 breeding pairs of Royal Penguins, about 400,000

It is estimated there are 1,700,000 Royal Penguins on Macquarie Island.

King Penguin
Southern Rockhopper Penguin
Antarctic Tern
AND, PERHAPS THE
MOST DIFFICULT:
Common Redpoll

breeding pairs of Southern Rockhopper Penguins (the smallest penguin on Macquarie), 100,000 breeding pairs of the spectacular King Penguins, and about 5,000 breeding pairs of Gentoo Penguins.

Apart from the penguins, there are other delights for the birder on Macquarie. There are Antarctic Terns, Macquarie Shags, Northern and Southern Giant Petrels (including the white morph of the latter), Brown Skuas, Kelp Gulls and four species of Albatross: Black-browed, Grey-headed, Light-mantled and Wandering. There are Mottled and Soft-plumaged Petrels around about too.

And then there's the Common Redpoll. Macquarie Island is the easiest place to get this European bird onto your Australian list. (Redpolls have been reported from Lord Howe Island, but I wouldn't want to rely on seeing them there.) Redpolls were introduced to New Zealand by homesick 19th-century Britons. Sweet little things (the Redpolls, not the Britons), they are smaller than a sparrow. Yet they managed to get to Macquarie Island from New Zealand by themselves – a trip of some 1,200 kilometres. Not a bad effort for such a small bird,

you might think. But, consider that at home in Europe, they may spend summer in Iceland and winter in the south of France – a journey twice as long as from New Zealand to Macquarie Island – and they do it every year – and back again!

Visiting Macquarie was truly amazing, with many memorable moments: witnessing the ballet that is the mating flight of Light-mantled Albatross; identifying a vagrant Chinstrap Penguin; seeing my first iceberg; and finally ticking the exotic Common Redpoll. I found the conditions difficult, but the penguins alone were worth any minor discomfort.

Gentoo Penguins, the least numerous of the penguins found reliably on Macquarie Island, are very endearing.

Chiltern's two dams are known as 'Number One' and 'Number Two'. This is Number Two.

Chiltern

Chiltern is famous for Regent Honeyeaters and Turquoise Parrots, two most sought-after species. It is located just off the Hume Freeway, three and a half hours north of Melbourne.

At the Chiltern Visitor Information Centre, you can pick up a free brochure entitled *Bird Trails of Chiltern* written by Barry Traill and published by the Chiltern Tourism Association. It will tell you where to look for Spotted Quail-thrush and Grey-crowned Babblers, and lists all the best birdy spots. Greenhill Dam is a must – this is where I saw my first Regent Honeyeaters. Two other dams, imaginatively called 'Number One Dam' and 'Number Two Dam', are always worth a visit.

There is a roadside stop on the freeway called 'Chiltern Park'. It's before you get to Chiltern, if you are coming from the north. Here, motorists are encouraged to 'Take A Walk' and deluded into thinking that the walking track will take only 15 minutes to

Regent Honeyeaters are exceptionally handsome and exceptionally difficult to find.

complete. Chiltern Park is an absolute delight for birders. It is actually part of the Chiltern Box-Ironbark National Park. Despite being so close to the noise of the freeway, it is a little oasis of birdy heaven. The track meanders around a picturesque dam where you'll see lots of honeyeaters, whistlers, thornbills, pardalotes, robins, Silvereyes and Brown Treecreepers.

There's another roadside stop, also north of Chiltern, on the other side of the freeway, called 'Ironbark'. It is just a standard VicRoads car park with toilets and picnic tables. There is no adjacent national park, but, as its name suggests, it has the advantage of many ironbarks, so it's a good spot to look for Regent Honeyeaters. I've seen them here just once.

After Chiltern Park, my two favourite spots are Bartley's Block and Cyanide Dam. Bartley's Block is about three kilometres north of town on the

road to Howlong. I usually see Red-capped Robins, Turquoise Parrots, Rufous Whistlers, Jacky Winters, Mistletoebirds, Restless Flycatchers and lots of honeyeaters. In summer I sometimes hear Painted Honeyeaters making their distinctive 'George-ee' call. They are more easily heard than seen. Once, during the drought, I saw a Rufous Fantail here. Grey Fantails are common and there are sometimes Nankeen Night Herons at the dam.

Cyanide Dam is in Honeyeater Picnic Area in the national park. It's called Honeyeater Picnic Area for good reason: the honeyeaters are prolific here. The walk around the dam has recently been upgraded and now is safe to do while you're distracted looking up into the flowering white box admiring Musk Lorikeets, or perhaps Sacred Kingfishers or Oriental Dollarbirds. I've seen both Swift and Turquoise Parrots here, and watched Fuscous Honeyeaters, Willie Wagtails, Spotted Pardalotes and Brown Treecreepers nesting. Just once I've seen Gang-gang Cockatoos and, also just once, a koala. There are always Eastern Yellow Robins and Brown Treecreepers and usually White-browed Babblers.

We Victorians are very lucky to have Chiltern: truly, a birder's paradise.

Turquoise Parrot
Painted Buttonquail
Rufous Songlark (summer)
AND, IF YOU'RE VERY LUCKY
Regent Honeyeater

Turquoise Parrots are gorgeous and, although they are not rare at Chiltern, they are surprisingly easily overlooked.

Lamington National Park

It's worth going to Lamington National Park just for the Regent Bowerbirds. The spectacular black-and-gold males are common around O'Reilly's Guesthouse, located in the middle of the park. Other birding highlights include Albert's Lyrebird, Satin Bowerbirds, Paradise Riflebirds and, so they tell me, Rufous Scrubbirds. The less said about this reprobate the better.

Lamington National Park is in the McPherson Range on the border of New South Wales and Queensland, 120 kilometres south of Brisbane. It comprises 20,200 hectares of subtropical and temperate rainforest. You can stay either at the aforementioned O'Reilly's Guesthouse in the middle of the park, or you can camp. Sadly, Binna Burra Mountain Lodge was destroyed in the 2019 bushfires and has not yet been rebuilt. Fires notwithstanding, most of Lamington remains intact and certainly deserves to be in my top ten birding sites.

At O'Reilly's Guesthouse there is a treetop walk that wobbles disconcertingly. I've only done it once and did not see any birds.

There are over 150 species on the Lamington bird list. As well as the Regent Bowerbirds, other gaudy birds include Noisy Pitta, Scaly-breasted Lorikeet

6

Despite its name, the Noisy Pitta is not particularly noisy, but it is certainly gorgeous.

Heyn de Kock

and Rose-crowned Fruit Dove. Equally exciting, but quieter, species include Pale Yellow Robin, Pale-headed Rosella, Topknot Pigeon and Bassian Thrush. There are always too many spiders and it often rains, but every day is different. One trip we made to Lamington was dominated by giant skinks. Once, in the rain, I was threatened by a very large spiny crayfish, waving his claws at me and guarding his puddle from intruders. On one walk, we lost count of the number of red-necked pademelons, while Green Catbirds and Eastern Whipbirds called incessantly. The following day, there were as many Australian Logrunners as there had been pademelons the day before.

There are Rose Robins and Olive Whistlers. Unassuming Pacific Emerald Doves walk quietly by, while ostentatious Eastern Spinebills are a flurry of activity, ensuring that they are noticed. Australian Brushturkeys are too big to be overlooked and if Varied Trillers are trilling, they cannot be missed.

There are more birds in summer when the cuckoos and monarchs come visiting. There are Brush and Fan-tailed Cuckoos and Pacific Koels, and Black-faced and Spectacled Monarchs.

However, Lamington National Park is worth visiting at any time of year. After all, the Regent Bowerbirds are resident all year round.

Lamington National Park comprises over 20,000 hectares of subtropical and temperate rainforest.

Regent Bowerbirds will sometimes eat cheese out of your hand.

Regent Bowerbird
Albert's Lyrebird
Australian Logrunner
Green Catbird

Cocos (Keeling) Islands

I've visited the Cocos Islands four times and seen a remarkable 28 lifers there. (Lifers are birds you see for the first time in your life – a noteworthy experience.) Three of these visits occurred after I wrote the first edition of this book. That is why Cocos did not appear. It certainly deserves a spot in Australia's top 100 birdwatching sites. In fact (as you see) I believe it is in the top ten. Birders go to Cocos again and again looking for rare vagrants. You don't know what you'll see but chances are something rare will turn up. Either a Mugimaki Flycatcher or a Common Kingfisher or a Watercock. In early 2017 a single Barau's Petrel turned up at the airport on West Island. It returned again in 2018. Alas, not when I was there.

Cocos (Keeling) Islands are 2,700 kilometres north-north-west of Perth in the Indian Ocean. There are two coral atolls comprising 27 islands, only two of which are inhabited. About 400 people of Malay extraction live on Home Island and about 200 people mainly of European extraction on West Island. There is a regular ferry service between the two islands.

The ferry will also take you to Horsburgh Island where you can see the local endemic race of Buff-banded Rail, and Christmas White-eye (Cocos Islands' only resident passerine), but you must arrange other transport to South Island to see Saunders's Tern. Access to North Keeling Island (24 kilometres north) is by swimming only. The entire island is a national park, and you must be taken by an approved guide. In 1988 a Greater Flamingo was seen on North Keeling – the only record for Australia, apart from fossil records from Lake Eyre.

Cocos Islands were discovered in 1609, but were not settled until 1826 when John Clunies-Ross brought Malay labourers to Home Island to grow coconuts. His grandson built a mansion, officially called Oceania House, but locally known as the Big House. Birders go there because vagrants often turn up in the gardens. I've seen both a Siberian and an Eyebrowed Thrush, a Black-crowned Night Heron and a Chestnut-winged Cuckoo. I've seen a Javan Pond Heron in the coconut plantation and a Chinese Pond Heron at Pulu Ampang, which involved a very

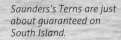

Saunders's Terns are just about guaranteed on South Island.

White-breasted Waterhen are very common and very cute.

long, very scary wade through waist deep water. I earnt that bird!

I've seen Asian Koels on both Home and West Islands. Nowadays birders are guaranteed both White Terns and White-breasted Waterhens. Waterherns were not guaranteed on my first visit in 2007. There will be Oriental Pratincoles on the airport runway. Here I've seen both a Red-throated and a Tree Pipit, as well as Von Schrenk's Bittern. I've seen Yellow Bitterns at the bottle dump and an Asian Brown Flycatcher at Trannies Beach. Everyone visits the swamp known as Bechat Besar and the nearby farm. At Bechat Besar I've seen Eurasian Teal, Chinese Sparrowhawks and Northern Pintail. At the farm, I've seen a Brown Shrike and a Square-tailed Drongo-Cuckoo.

Quite a remarkable list of vagrants, I'm sure you'll agree. The scenery is picture postcard perfect and with birds such as I've mentioned, it is well worth making the effort to travel to the Cocos Islands.

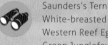
Saunders's Tern
White-breasted Waterhen
Western Reef Egret
Green Junglefowl

Cocos is full of quintessentially pretty scenery. This is a view from West Island.

Macleay's Honeyeaters come to the birdfeeders at Julatten, giving great views for birdwatchers.

Julatten

Some years ago on our first visit to Julatten, Rog was sitting on the verandah. He called me over to see a Chestnut-breasted Cuckoo that had landed in a tree right in front of him. I hurried out, but inevitably, when I arrived, the bird had gone. Instead, I saw an Olive-backed Sunbird being escorted by two gorgeous Ulysses butterflies. How could I possibly complain about missing out on a cuckoo?

We were staying at Kingfisher Park Birdwatchers Lodge, one of my very favourite places. Of course I love this spot. I've seen at least five lifers here: Superb Fruit Dove, Red-necked Crake, Buff-breasted Paradise-Kingfisher, Yellow-breasted Boatbill and Blue-faced Parrotfinch. What a scintillating assembly of birds! And all except the parrotfinch were actually in the grounds of the lodge.

Julatten is at the northern end of the Atherton Tablelands in far north Queensland. It is 110 kilometres (or one and a half hours' drive) north-west of Cairns, and Kingfisher Park Birdwatchers Lodge is the place to stay. The bird list comprises a phenomenal 265 species. This includes 25 honeyeaters, 20 raptors, 12 pigeons and 11 cuckoos.

There are both Australian Brushturkeys and Orange-footed Scrubfowl scratching in the grounds. Rufous Owls can sometimes be seen roosting by day. Night walks often reveal Masked, Eastern Barn and Lesser Sooty Owls as well as spectacled flying-foxes.

You can see Blue-winged Kookaburras at Julatten, but Laughing Kookaburras are more common.

Red-necked Crakes are probably most easily seen at Kingfisher Park.

Kingfisher Park is named after the truly stunning Buff-breasted Paradise-Kingfisher that arrives from New Guinea each October and, displaying excellent taste, stays to breed in the grounds.

Red-necked Crake and Pacific Emerald Dove wander around the garden. Macleay's Honeyeaters, wearing their most attractive eye make-up, are common at the water bowls. Pale-vented Bush-hen can sometimes be seen by the creek as you watch for platypus. On your way to the creek, look out for Fairy Gerygones, Spectacled Monarchs and Pale Yellow Robins. Yellow-breasted Boatbills are also common and not difficult to see. Perhaps not quite so colourful, but nonetheless desirable, both Grey-headed Robins and Grey Whistlers can be seen here. Great Bowerbirds are round about too. For many years there was a bower easily accessible in the nearby school yard.

Chowchillas are common, as are Rufous Shrikethrush. Barred Cuckooshrikes are not common, but can be seen here on occasion. Flocks of Double-eyed Fig Parrots zoom overhead, drawing attention to themselves with constant high-pitched staccato screeches. Channel-billed Cuckoos, with their grotesquely outsized bills, have a more laboured flight and a more raucous voice.

There's always something special somewhere at Kingfisher Park Birdwatchers Lodge.

Buff-breasted Paradise-Kingfisher
Macleay's Honeyeater
Spectacled Monarch
AND, IF YOU'RE LUCKY
Red-necked Crake

Magpie Geese are most unusual birds. The knob on their head gets larger with age. These birds are quite young, as their knobs are barely noticeable.

Townsville Town Common Conservation Park

Watching Brolgas dancing is a breathtaking experience for anyone – you don't have to be a birder. How such big birds can be so very graceful is astounding. And the Townsville Town Common is a great place to watch them.

The second most obvious bird on the Common is the quirky Magpie Goose, so unusual ornithologists have placed it in a family all by itself. It has half-webbed feet, a strong hooked bill and an unusual knob on its head that grows larger as the birds age. Magpie Geese are breeding residents on Townsville's Town Common; there are tens of thousands of them.

The Town Common is about six kilometres north of Townsville, which is 1,350 kilometres north of Brisbane. It is open every day from 6.30 am until 6.30 pm. The Common is 3,245 hectares and is of international importance for waterbirds. Maps can

Brolgas are always beautiful. Check the amount of red on the head to ensure they're not Sarus Cranes.

be obtained from the ranger station, along with a bird list that includes an impressive 280 species.

Apart from the iconic Brolgas and Magpie Geese, the most common waterbirds are pelicans, Black-necked Storks and Pacific Black Ducks. There are both Little Pied and Little Black Cormorants and there are always White-necked Herons. For those of us who always need help honing our identification skills, it's helpful to be able to see Great Egrets adjacent to Intermediate and Little Egrets. (Look at the neck length, head shape, bill colour and extent of gape.) Comb-crested Jacanas are common too – how special is that?

Not quite so abundant are Wandering Whistling Duck, Nankeen Night Heron and Pale-vented Bush-hen. This must surely be the southern limit for White-browed Crake, which I always think of as belonging to the very far north of the continent. It is also possible to see both Cotton and Green Pygmy Geese. Cotton Pygmy Geese seem to be getting harder to see and it's good to know that they're still seen occasionally at the Townsville Town Common.

While the Common is of international significance for waterbirds, the site also includes some eucalypt woodlands, rainforest and mangroves, so there are good bush birds too. There are Blue-winged Kookaburras and Little Kingfishers (it must be about their southern limit too). There are 18 species of honeyeater on the bird list, the most common being Brown-backed, Brown, Yellow, White-throated and Hornbill Friarbird.

There are Red-backed Fairywrens, Olive-backed Sunbirds and Spangled Drongos. In winter, there are Australian Bustards and White-eared Monarchs.

The bird list really is extensive. I've only mentioned species that are common. Although, I must say that Brolgas alone would satisfy me. Especially if they danced.

Magpie Goose
Pheasant Coucal
Brown-backed Honeyeater
AND, IF YOU'RE LUCKY
Cotton Pygmy Goose

The romance of sunset at the Townsville Town Common is enhanced by a duck and an egret.

Shy Albatrosses are possible off
Kiama at any time of year.

Kiama
pelagic

I can't believe that an experience I
dread so intently has not only made
it onto my list of top birding sites, but
has actually squeaked into the top ten.

'Pelagic' is an adjective meaning
'pertaining to the open sea'. Birders incorrectly
use this adjective as a noun, to mean 'a boat trip out
to sea looking for seabirds'. Every time I book to go
on a pelagic, I am filled with childish enthusiasm.
I'm sure that I'm going to see a Juan Fernandez
Petrel or an Audubon's Shearwater. I just know
that there's something special out there waiting
for me. As the trip grows nearer and I study my
books and my lists, nagging doubts begin to gnaw
at me. I begin to realise that we probably won't get
anything rare. I'll fall over in front of everyone
and make an idiot of myself. I'll drop my binoculars
overboard and give everyone a good laugh.

The first obstacle is getting onto the boat. Kiama
pelagics go out on the *M. V. Kato*, which is a fishing
boat. It is not designed to be accessible for women of
a certain age. Having managed to clamber aboard,
I attempt to sit quietly and unobtrusively, hiding
my incompetence and my ignorance. Once we're
out at sea, the boat lurches and pitches and plunges.
Under these impossible conditions, the pelagic
experts on board
can separate Sooty
from Short-tailed Shearwaters – something
mere mortals have difficulty doing under ideal
circumstances. They can identify a species of
albatross before I can see the bird!

I find it impossible to focus my binoculars
while the boat is moving. I hang on for dear
life. Someone's always seasick, and, from time
to time throughout the day, passengers are
engulfed in freezing seawater. Then, when you're
at your most queasy, the crew pours some fragrant
fish oil into the water to attract the birds.

Perversely, birding out of Kiama remains one of
my top birding experiences. That is predominantly
because of Lindsay Smith and the Southern Oceans
Seabird Study Association. SOSSA runs the Kiama
pelagics and usually does some banding while
they're out at sea. It's great watching shearwaters
and even albatrosses being caught with an outsized
butterfly net.

If you want to know more about SOSSA, check
out the website: <www.sossa-international.org/>.
You can time your trip according to what you want
to see. Wedge-tailed, Flesh-footed and Short-tailed
Shearwaters, and Pomarine and Parasitic Jaegers
are very common from October until April. Yellow-
nosed Albatross and Brown Skuas are common
from June until September. Black-browed Albatross
are common from June until November. Shy
Albatross are common from July until November.
White-faced Storm Petrels are always frequent and
Fluttering Shearwaters are always very common.
Of course, the rare ones can turn up at any time.

SOSSA runs pelagics out of Kiama on the fourth Saturday of every month.

A White-faced Storm Petrel patters past a Wandering Albatross.

Fluttering Shearwater
Pomarine Jaeger
Wandering Albatross
AND, IF YOU'RE VERY LUCKY
White-necked Petrel (summer)

11 Darwin

Is any bird more beautiful than the Rainbow Pitta? When I think of Rainbow Pittas, I think of Darwin. There are other great birds around Darwin too, such as Rufous Owls, Beach Stone-curlews and Lemon-bellied Flyrobins.

Birders go to the Darwin Botanic Gardens looking for Rufous Owls. I shudder to recall how many times I visited the gardens before I was successful. And when I finally did see my Rufous Owl, I thought it looked small compared with its big Queensland cousin. In fact, the text books tell us that the Top End bird is significantly larger than either of the eastern races. I find it fascinating that,

Rainbow Pittas are stunning little birds, even if they don't display all the colours of the rainbow.

Leanyer sewerage treatment ponds are highly recommended. You'll see some great birds if you can put up with the heat.

with the best will in the world, it's possible for observations to be quite misleading.

On unsuccessful owl hunts, I had to make do with admiring Orange-footed Scrubfowl scratching in the undergrowth. I do adore their cheeky hairdo! Then there are colourful Australasian Figbirds, speedy White-gaped Honeyeaters and, best of all, magnificent Rainbow Pittas.

Pittas are gloriously coloured ground birds. They are so brightly coloured I'm always amazed how well they can hide in the rainforest. I remember well

The thick bill of this Greater Sand Plover, is, I think, the best way to identify it from its Lesser relation.

Rainbow Pitta
Rufous Owl
Mangrove Gerygone
White-gaped Honeyeater

my first Rainbow Pitta. It was at East Point. The bird tantalized me. I could hear him calling, a call very similar to the 'walk to work' call of the Noisy Pitta. I followed the call, but I couldn't find the bird. I stood bemused, wondering where he was hiding. Roger said he was in a tree. I looked, and sure enough, there he was, my ground bird, perched high in a tree, proclaiming his presence to the world.

We saw Pacific Koels, too, that day and, along the boardwalk through the mangroves we saw stunning White-breasted Whistlers and a tiny Lemon-bellied Flyrobin sitting on the tiniest possible nest – in fact, it is the smallest nest in the bird world.

There are also Mangrove and Green-backed Gerygones, and Brown and Rufous-banded Honeyeaters. Pacific Reef Herons stalk the shore and ubiquitous Masked Lapwings loiter with intent. Rose-crowned Fruit Doves sit up high and are so quiet that they are often overlooked.

In the southern states, we look forward to Rainbow Bee-eaters arriving to give our summer a splash of colour. Lucky Territorians can enjoy bee-eaters all year round.

On our first trip to Darwin, we visited the tip looking for Barn Swallows. Instead, we saw dozens of Pied Herons, Australian White Ibis and Whistling Kites.

At Doctors Gully, we saw Beach Stone-curlew, Northern Fantails, Buff-sided Robins (which, in those days, we called White-browed Robins) and a Striated Heron sitting on her nest looking most uncomfortable. Any exciting wader could fly in. Birds that we see rarely in the south, such as Greater Sand Plovers, are seen here regularly.

When I'm in Darwin, I try to fit in a trip to the Leanyer sewage treatment ponds. Of course there are lots of waterfowl, and always the chance of a rarity. Last time I was there, I scored a Little Ringed Plover.

Darwin might be hot and sticky, but what's a bit of discomfort when you can see Rainbow Pittas and Rufous Owls?

This Pied Stilt is more interested in feeding than admiring its own reflection.

There are some most tantalizing birds on the Ash Island list. Birds like Comb-crested Jacana, Pheasant Coucal and Ruff. The truth is you are more likely to see Australasian Swamphen, Black-faced Cuckooshrike and Yellow Thornbill. You will certainly see swans and ducks, herons and ibis, Masked Lapwings and, my favourite bird, the Willie Wagtail. I'd be surprised if you didn't see Pied Stilt.

There is a good chance, too, of seeing Mangrove Gerygones. Access to the island is by a bridge. As soon as you cross the bridge, stop at the car park. Mangrove Gerygones can be seen around here. I saw my first Mangrove Gerygone near Darwin and had always thought of them as living in the far north of the continent. Indeed, Ash Island is about as far south as they come. While they are associated with mangroves, they are more often found in adjacent paperbarks.

In summer, all the usual suspects turn up from the northern hemisphere. You will find sandpipers (Common, Curlew, Marsh and Sharp-tailed), godwits (both Bar-tailed and Black-tailed), Common Greenshank and Pacific Golden Plovers. And of course there are flocks of sweet little Red-necked Stints. These birds only weigh 25 grams. It is incredible to think of them breeding in Siberia or Alaska then coming to spend summer with us. That's about 8,000 kilometres – if they fly in a straight line.

With all these wonderful birds, I couldn't be disappointed at missing out on grass owls. And there are so many I haven't mentioned, like dotterels, crakes and chats.

Ignore the inappropriate name and make an effort to visit Ash Island in February, when you just might see Eastern Yellow Wagtails.

Ash Island

Ash Island is a total misnomer. The ash trees that once grew here are no longer extant and it is no longer an island. Several estuarine islands were amalgamated for industrial development, and what is known as 'Ash Island' is the western end of Kooragang Island. It is located 12 kilometres west of Newcastle on the central New South Wales coast. Whatever you call it, Ash Island is a very special place for waterbirds. It is probably most famous for Eastern Yellow Wagtails, which turn up in February and leave in early March.

I was very excited to learn that Ash Island was home to Eastern Grass Owls until I discovered how difficult they were to see. I had more chance of seeing Magpie Geese, Black-necked Storks, Brahminy Kites and Pectoral Sandpipers.

Eastern Yellow Wagtail (February)
Brahminy Kite
Mangrove Gerygone
AND, IF YOU'RE LUCKY
Eastern Grass Owl

This Black-tailed Godwit still has some breeding colour. Note the straight bill.

Ash Island has both resident waders (such as these Red-necked Avocets) and migratory visitors (like these godwits).

Australian Pratincoles are common around Lake Argyle.

Lake Argyle

When you are in the eastern Kimberley, you must make time to visit Lake Argyle. About 40 minutes' drive from Kununurra, the lake is of national significance for waterbirds. A breakfast boat tour is highly recommended.

Birders come here to see Yellow Chats. You can see them elsewhere (Broome, Barkly Tableland, Derby) but, in my experience, you'll get much closer views at Lake Argyle.

This is a huge body of water – some 2,000 square kilometres. It is Australia's biggest lake. There are many islands with White-quilled Rock Pigeons and Sandstone Shrikethrush on each. When we did the boat tour, we were watched from each island by inquisitive short-eared rock-wallabies. There were Australian Pelicans and Australian Pied Cormorants aplenty and Wandering Whistling Ducks, Pacific Black Ducks and Comb-crested Jacana playing on the water. White-bellied Sea Eagles sat, aloof, in dead trees, surveying their kingdom. At the water's edge, there were Glossy Ibis, Black-necked Stork, Great Egret and Black-fronted Dotterels. Paperbark Flycatchers chattered happily and Long-tailed Finches hopped in the grass. And I mustn't forget the Torresian Crow. It's so nice to be somewhere in Australia where there's only one corvid and you don't have to worry about the correct identification.

While there are many islands, the breakfast boat tour lands at one the guide has named 'Chat Island'. In fact, we saw male and female Yellow Chats before we disembarked. He is indeed a gorgeous bird. From the boat I could see Brolgas, Australian Bustards, Australian Pratincole, Magpie-larks and Red-capped Plovers. I considered staying on board while the others explored the island – after all, I'd already seen my chats. Of course, I couldn't bear the possibility of missing out on something, so, reluctantly, I took off my shoes and lowered myself awkwardly down the ladder at the back of the boat.

The water was only ankle-deep, but it was full of slimy weeds. I wished I'd stayed on board. But then we saw a Long-toed Stint and I forgot my self-absorption. Then we saw a Reeve and I stopped thinking about having to wade back through the water to return to the boat later. By the time we saw an Oriental Plover, the island had won me over completely. Then the Little Curlew was icing on the cake. Other birds we saw on that island included: Common Greenshank, Whiskered and Australian Tern (which, at the time, we called Gull-billed Tern), Curlew, Sharp-tailed, Wood and Marsh Sandpiper, Buff-banded Rail, Horsfield's Bush Lark and a Nankeen Night Heron.

I'd say it was worth getting my feet wet, wouldn't you?

Covering 2000 square kilometres, Lake Argyle is Australia's biggest lake.

Birdwatchers everywhere delight in seeing a Little Curlew.

Yellow Chat
White-quilled Rock Pigeon
Sandstone Shrikethrush
Australian Pratincole

Eastern Yellow Robins nest at Kooyoora – as do Hooded and Red-capped Robins.

Kooyoora State Park

14 I love north central Victoria's dry, open box-ironbark forest. And I love the huge granite boulders scattered throughout the landscape. Spectacular orchids decorate the countryside in spring and summer, and here you find some of Australia's best birds, such as Crested Bellbirds, Gilbert's Whistlers, Hooded Robins and Southern Whiteface.

Kooyoora State Park, 205 kilometres north-west of Melbourne, is home to Melville Caves. Take the Calder Highway to Inglewood, turn west and you'll find Melville Caves 21 kilometres further on. There aren't really any caves. Just large cavities among the boulders, where the bushranger Captain Melville had his hide-out. High on the hill, it would have been a good lookout for him. Wedge-tailed Eagles nest here and Laughing Kookaburras frequent the picnic ground.

The eerie whistle of White-winged Choughs echoes through the forest, while Diamond Firetails hop in the grass. The Spotted Pardalotes here are the race called Yellow-rumped and I think they're even more colourful than the nominate race. Always in friendly family parties, the White-browed Babblers chatter and whistle and miaow to each other playfully. They build huge, untidy, bottle-shaped nests and use them for communal roosting as well as breeding.

There are four cuckoos on the Melville Caves bird list, including the Black-eared. And there are an impressive 19 honeyeaters, including the White-fronted Chat. During drought, you can see White-fronted Honeyeaters here too. Three thornbills are common and all must nest here, but I've only ever found the nest of Chestnut-rumped. The others are Yellow and Yellow-rumped.

Painted Honeyeaters are quite common from October to March, and Spiny-cheeked are always common. One January, I lost count of the number of Spiny-cheeked's nests I found – all in gum trees and all conveniently at eye level. New Hollands are probably the most common honeyeater – they are certainly the most prominent. I've found their nests in every month of the year. White-plumed and Fuscous are also common, as are Red Wattlebirds. There are also Black-chinned and White-naped and, one of my favourites, Brown-headed.

One November, there was an irruption of Woodswallows. Every scraggly wattle was home to a nest of a White-browed and every eucalypt housed a Dusky's nest.

To celebrate Roger's birthday on 24 October, the summer migrants start to arrive. First come Painted Honeyeaters, Mistletoebirds and gorgeous Rainbow Bee-eaters, followed later by White-winged Trillers, Rufous Songlarks and Olive-backed Orioles.

Meanwhile, Restless Flycatchers continue to grind their scissors and both White-throated and Brown Treecreepers keep creeping up the trees.

Little Lorikeets nest high in the grey box. Musk and Purple-crowned Lorikeets are common too, but I haven't found their nests. Three robins breed here each summer: Hooded, Red-capped and Eastern Yellow. Scarlet and Flame Robins pass through disdainfully, preferring to nest in the mountains.

It can be hot in summer and cold in winter, but this is beautiful country and the birds are phenomenal.

Several thornbills call Kooyoora home. Chestnut-rumped Thornbills nest here each year.

Known to the locals as 'lizard country', Kooyoora State Park provides wonderful birdwatching.

Painted Honeyeater (summer)
Black-eared Cuckoo (summer)
Southern Whiteface
Diamond Firetail

15 The Rock Nature Reserve – Kengal Aboriginal Place

We found The Rock Nature Reserve quite by accident. We were on our way home from Wagga Wagga and just happened to notice it. You can't miss The Rock itself. It stands proudly, the one rugged feature on a flat plain, clearly visible from a great distance.

The township of The Rock has a thriving population of 1,000, and a grandiose main street wider than any capital city boulevard I know. It's on the Olympic Highway 25 kilometres south of Wagga Wagga, 96 kilometres north of Albury. The nature reserve is 3.5 kilometres west of the township and comprises 350 hectares of beautiful bush.

The reserve has a large car park and covered picnic tables where Roger would read his newspaper while I admired the sittellas and the babblers.

I love this sort of open eucalypt woodland with grey box, Blakely's red gum, white box and the occasional white cypress-pine. They tell me that the vegetation changes higher up and the white box dominates. I can't vouch for that. I've never ventured up The Rock. It is 250 metres high, making it 570 metres above sea level. A sign invites you to venture up the Yerong Nature Track. It is six kilometres and takes three hours. The sign coyly admits that it is 'steep'. In my experience, when signage that's supposed to encourage you to explore a reserve uses a word like 'steep', I know that, for me, it's quite impassable. Anyway, why would anyone bother to go rock climbing when the birds are so good down below?

Not even the promise of spectacular views of the snow-capped peak of Mount Kosciuszko could lure me up there. They say that Peregrine Falcons and Wedge-tailed Eagles nest up high on The Rock, but the only raptors I've ever seen in the reserve are a Square-tailed Kite and a Brown Goshawk.

I'm surprised The Rock doesn't feature in other people's lists of top birding sites. It has never let me down. I've never been there without seeing something exciting, although I've never seen a Turquoise Parrot or a Glossy Black Cockatoo, which are both on the bird list. I always see Speckled Warblers, Red-capped Robins, Brown Treecreepers, Chestnut-rumped Thornbills, Apostlebirds and sometimes a Leaden Flycatcher. I've also seen Western Gerygones and Peaceful Doves and a Crested Shriketit chasing a Jacky Winter.

Let's face it, anywhere you can reliably see Speckled Warblers has to number among your top birding sites.

Male Red-capped Robins are showy, but females are exceptionally pretty, as this photo demonstrates.

Speckled Warbler
Red-capped Robin
Peaceful Dove
Brown-headed Honeyeater

I've never visited The Rock
without seeing Speckled
Warblers. These beautiful
little birds are very common
here. The chestnut stripe over
her eye shows she is female.

You can't miss The Rock:
it stands out from a great
distance.

An Australian Owlet-nightjar can sometimes be seen in a eucalypt hollow.

Banyule Flats Reserve

16

Right smack bang in the middle of suburbia, Banyule Flats Reserve is about 13 kilometres from central Melbourne. If you are visiting Melbourne with restricted time, after you've been to Werribee, this is your next port of call. Apart from a couple of sports ovals and cricket nets, Banyule boasts a swamp, wetlands and some wonderful remnant bush along the Yarra River. The Banyule bird list includes 148 species, both waterbirds and bush birds.

I discovered Banyule in October 2001 when a female Australian Painted-snipe turned up here. In the days before GPS, the Melway reference (32 F2) was on the internet immediately and twitchers followed by the carload. That cooperative snipe hung around for weeks and patient birders were rewarded with great sightings. As far as I know, she hasn't been back since.

Latham's Snipe visit every summer and you can see crakes and cute fluffy moorhen chicks. There's usually a Grey Butcherbird fluting his musical song in the car park. Musk Lorikeets forage in the flowering gumtrees and you are sure to see Noisy Miners and Crested Pigeons. New Holland Honeyeaters are common, as are Sulphur-crested Cockatoos, and Rainbow Lorikeets squawk overhead. You may even flush a Buff-banded Rail.

Depending on the season and the water levels, the best birding may be at the swamp, where an optimistic sign features a bittern. I've seen koalas and snakes and wombat droppings, but I have never seen a bittern here. Some old dead trees stand in the water and there's often something interesting perched in them, perhaps an Australian Hobby, perhaps Little Corellas. There are usually swans and ducks and coots and grebes, Little Pied Cormorants, Silver Gulls and Australian White Ibis. Once there was an enormous flock of Eastern Cattle Egrets.

There are two seats where you can sit and contemplate the water, while the Crested Shriketits call overhead. I've met some interesting people sitting on those seats. On 1 January each year, twitchers trying to start their year off with a bang often pass this way and are always a great source of birdy gossip.

If you walk beside the Yarra to where the Plenty River flows into it, there is a footbridge over the tributary. Pause on this footbridge and look closely at the holes in the gumtrees over the water. There is sometimes an Australian Owlet-nightjar here.

In the bush you'll see Spotted Pardalotes and, in summer, Mistletoebirds and Olive-backed Orioles are plentiful. Rufous and Australian Golden Whistlers are common. By the river you're guaranteed to hear the tinkling call of Bell Miners, and Powerful Owls are often seen roosting in dense vegetation. Only once have I seen Gang-gang Cockatoos. I was alerted to their presence by their distinctive growly croaks.

Is it any wonder that overseas birders put Banyule Flats Reserve high on their priority list when they're visiting Melbourne?

Banyule Flats Reserve, right in the middle of suburbia, boasts a bird list of 148 species.

Latham's Snipe (summer)
Grey Butcherbird
Tawny Frogmouth
AND, IF YOU'RE LUCKY
Australian Owlet-nightjar

Latham's Snipe visit Banyule every summer.

Seas can be rough off Eaglehawk Neck, but the albatrosses make the discomfort worthwhile.

17 Eaglehawk Neck pelagic

I hate pelagics and yet, remarkably, three have made it onto my top 100 birding sites. I've met some fascinating people on little boats out at sea. It's as if, having endured such torture together, we have a common bond. Tasmanian pelagics are invariably very cold and the seas can be very rough. But you can see some wonderful birds off Tasmania that you are unlikely to see off the mainland. Birds like Broad-billed Prions, Grey Petrels and Southern Fulmars. Eaglehawk Neck is on Tasmania's east coast, 80 kilometres east of Hobart. My boat of preference is the *Pauletta*. Rohan Clarke organizes pelagics out of Eaglehawk Neck. His email is ehnpelagics@gmail.com.

On summer trips out of Eaglehawk Neck, I've seen Mottled, Gould's, Cook's and White-chinned Petrels and Buller's Shearwaters. I've only seen Soft-plumaged Petrels in November. I've seen White-headed Petrels from June to November. Prions and Blue Petrels (who like to hang around together) are best seen in winter. Brown Skuas and Common Diving Petrels are seen all year round, as are Grey-backed Storm Petrels, Great-winged Petrels and Northern Giant Petrels. I've seen Sooty Shearwaters on every Tasmanian pelagic I've ever done, and Fairy Prions on every trip out of Eaglehawk Neck. I've seen both races of Cape Petrels in winter and spring.

In my (admittedly very limited) experience, jaegers are not common off Tasmania.

As to the albatrosses, I've always seen Wandering, Black-browed and Shy out of Tasmania. I've seen both Northern and Southern Royal as well as Buller's Albatrosses from February to September. Indian Yellow-nosed Albatross I've seen from June to November. I've never seen Grey-headed, Sooty or Light-mantled out of Eaglehawk Neck.

Apart from the very special birds and my equally interesting fellow passengers, there is absolutely nothing pleasant about a pelagic. The boat heaves and pitches. Someone is always seasick. The stink of the berley (smelly stuff thrown overboard to attract the birds) makes everyone a little queasy. Off Eaglehawk Neck it is always uncomfortably cold. And you're a prisoner on that boat. If you've had enough by half past 11, you can't say 'take me back now'. You're committed for the whole day. The boat will turn back when the captain says and not before. Captains are quite unaware of their (paying) passengers' level of comfort. If I knew that there was no chance of a lifer, I'd never board a small boat.

But there is always that thrilling possibility of a rare bird. This will be the trip when a Fulmar Prion flies by. Today a South Georgian Diving Petrel will cavort in front of the boat. Atlantic Petrels will flock to the berley. And this thrilling possibility only ever becomes a reality when I'm not on the boat.

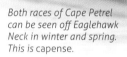

Both races of Cape Petrel can be seen off Eaglehawk Neck in winter and spring. This is capense.

I've seen Wandering Albatross on every Tasmanian pelagic I've ever done.

Both Royal Albatrosses
Northern Giant Petrel
Grey-backed Storm Petrel
White-chinned Petrel

The highlight of a trip to Kakadu National Park is the Yellow Water Cruise.

18

Kakadu National Park

Think of Kakadu National Park, and waterfalls, crocodiles and Aboriginal rock art come to mind. Kakadu deserves a place in Australia's top birding sites because the bird list contains nearly 300 species. All five of the Northern Territory endemics occur here. Chestnut-quilled Rock Pigeons, White-lined Honeyeaters and Black-banded Fruit Doves are easily seen on the Gunlom escarpment while you're looking for White-throated Grasswren. Hooded Parrots are a possibility here too, although I found them easier at Edith Falls in Nitmiluk National Park near Katherine.

Kakadu National Park comprises 20,000 square kilometres on the Arnhem escarpment and includes wetlands of international significance. It is three hours' drive from Darwin, or two from Katherine. I have stayed at the Gagudju Crocodile Holiday Inn at Jabiru and the Gagudju Lodge at Cooinda (to do the Yellow Waters Cruise), but more recently we were accommodated at the Mary River Roadhouse, just outside the park, and I found this more friendly.

For such big birds, Great-billed Herons can be surprisingly difficult to see when they stand perfectly still.

Red-tailed Black Cockatoos are common at Kakadu and it is the easiest place to see Black-tailed Treecreepers. Birders like to see the red-faced form of the Partridge Pigeon, and the inland race of the Helmeted Friarbird. When I was last there (September 2009) the Kakadu woollybutt had prolific magnificent orange flowers, full of Silver-crowned Friarbirds.

At Nourlangie Rock we saw Little Woodswallows as well as Black-tailed Treecreepers, Spangled Drongos and Northern Fantails sitting up straight and erect unlike other fantails. Orange-footed Scrubfowl went about their scratching, ignoring us completely, and White-throated Honeyeaters were common in the canopy. We saw several Forest Kingfishers and lots of Black-banded Fruit Doves, making me wonder how I'd missed them on previous trips.

Look for the chestnut wing patch when you see Chestnut-quilled Rock Pigeons in flight.

The highlight of any trip to Kakadu must be the Yellow Waters Cruise. There are lots of Brolgas, Black-necked Storks and Magpie Geese. There are Green Pygmy Geese, Pacific Black Duck, Radjah Shelduck and both Plumed and Wandering Whistling Duck. Little Corellas are abundant and colourful Azure Kingfishers don't lose their allure because they are common. Watch for Wood Sandpipers, Glossy Ibis and Buff-banded Rail. Last time I was there, both the Masked Lapwings and the Comb-crested Jacanas had fluffy chicks. We saw Arafura Fantails (which are even brighter than their southern rufous relatives), Lemon-bellied Flyrobins and Shining Flycatchers. There's always the chance of a Great-billed Heron. My notes confirm that we saw 37 species on that boat trip.

Kakadu can be hot and humid and sometimes waterfalls without water can disappoint. But, without hesitation I recommend the Yellow Waters Cruise, and I know that birders will struggle up the Gunlom escarpment in search of White-throated Grasswren no matter what I say.

Black-banded Fruit Dove
Black-tailed Treecreeper
Northern Fantail
AND, IF YOU'RE VERY LUCKY
White-throated Grasswren

19

Houtman Abrolhos

I visited the Houtman Abrolhos islands to see Lesser Noddies, but I got a lot more out of it than just one tick.

I was moved by the bloody history of the place, fascinated with wallabies adapted to drink salt water, impressed by an extremely large python and overwhelmed with the beautiful birds.

The Houtman Abrolhos islands are located on the edge of the continental shelf 60 very rough kilometres west of Geraldton. Geraldton is 424 kilometres north of Perth. The Abrolhos comprise 122 islands scattered over 100 kilometres from north to south. They are in three main groups: Wallabi, Easter and Pelsaert. On that trip, I had three minor complaints: it was very windy the whole time I was there; I found the coral shale extremely difficult to walk on; and Australian sea lions loll on the beaches, catching the unwary birder by surprise.

Birders visit the Abrolhos islands to see Lesser Noddies.

My target species, the Lesser Noddy, did not let me down. There are about 120,000 of them on the Abrolhos. In fact, you will find this race nowhere else. The population is now believed to be stable and the species is classified as vulnerable. They were nesting in the Easter Group when I was there: thousands of them on healthy mangroves on Wooded Island and more on denuded mangroves on Morley Island. Groups of up to 50 noddies sat with wings outspread, enjoying the sunshine on top of bushes that produced delicious salty native grapes.

To help hone my identification skills, there were also thousands of very similar Brown Noddies on Pelsaert Island, along with huge colonies of Sooty Terns. Elsewhere, smaller numbers of Bridled and Roseate Terns were nesting, some with eggs, some with tiny fluffy chicks. In all, I recorded six species of terns as well as the two noddies. Those not already mentioned were Caspian, Greater Crested and Fairy. I believe I also saw Lesser Crested, but they are not on the official list and this is a little south of their accepted distribution, so I might be wrong.

I was disappointed I did not see the endemic race of Painted Buttonquail. Nor did I see Spotless Crakes, which are classified as very common in the mangroves. As compensation, while I was looking for crakes, I saw Bar-tailed Godwits, Great Knots and both Lesser and Greater Sand Plovers.

I was lucky to glimpse a Red-tailed Tropicbird on Morley Island. Despite featuring on the signs on the island, these birds are seldom seen here.

One of my most precious memories of the Abrolhos is the White-faced Storm Petrels attracted to our boat's lights overnight when we were moored at Pelsaert. There were several on deck when we arose in the morning and we released them carefully by hand. It was the first time I'd had such a close view of the transparent webbing between their toes. They were soft and beautiful and not at all afraid.

I travelled over 4,000 kilometres to see Lesser Noddies and they were worth every kilometre. The trip remains one of my best birding experiences, well justifying a spot in my top 20 sites.

The Houtman Abrolhos islands are home to hundreds of thousands of terns.

Lesser Noddy
Roseate Tern
Painted Buttonquail (race *scintillans*)
AND, IF YOU ARE VERY LUCKY
Red-tailed Tropicbird

Cheynes Beach

As pretty as a postcard, Cheynes Beach is the place to stay while you search for the three south-western endemic fiends: Noisy Scrubbird (easy), Western Bristlebird (not too difficult) and Black-throated Whipbird (almost impossible).

Tawny Frogmouths nest in the Cheynes Beach Caravan Park and there are always Carnaby's Black Cockatoos and Western Wattlebirds in the banksias. I've stayed there four times, because it's a great base to visit Waychinicup National Park and Two People's Bay. The first time I stayed, White-breasted Robins were common, and I had the easiest and best sightings I'd ever had of Southern Emu-wrens; the second time there were Red-eared Firetails around the office; the third time a family of Brown Quail were resident, walking past me quite unconcerned as I sat reading a book, three pretty little chicks hurrying to keep up with mum; and the fourth time I visited I finally saw the Black-throated Whipbird – a bird I'd spent a great deal of time looking for on each previous occasion. I could tick it off my list at last.

Cheynes Beach is 68 kilometres east of Albany in south-west Western Australia and is surrounded by Waychinicup National Park. The bird list contains 83 species. Brush Bronzewings are common, as they like the coastal heathland. The so-called Common ones are not so common. However, Silvereyes are common, as are Red Wattlebirds and Grey Fantails. You can see both New Holland and White-cheeked Honeyeaters, and Splendid and Red-winged Fairywrens. You'll also see Welcome Swallows, Red-capped Parrots and lots of kangaroos. I never tire of watching Western Spinebills; it's a shame they won't pause for my camera. I did attempt to photograph the beautiful scalloped back of a female western magpie – quite different from our eastern birds. On the beach you'll see Silver and Pacific Gulls, and Sooty Oystercatchers. There's a picnic table near the beach where people sit and watch Noisy Scrubbirds.

Once we visited in March and were plagued by March flies. Rog sat outside reading, slapping the irritating insects which fell dead at his feet. Enterprising Spotted Scrubwrens hopped in quickly for a free feed.

From the caravan park, a track takes you to Lookout Point, which overlooks Back Beach. This area is popular with quad bikes, but the emu-wrens don't mind the noise. You can see Bald Island from here, where several scrubbirds have been translocated, as insurance in case the small mainland population is affected by bush fire.

I spent most of my time at Cheynes Beach looking for Black-throated Whipbirds, which are easily heard but not so easily seen. Laughing Kookaburras often chortled at my lack of success, and once I encountered a disturbingly aggressive small olive snake that I did not identify.

Now I've finally seen my whipbird, I have no excuse to return to Cheynes Beach. I will probably manage to go anyway, to have another look at Red-eared Firetails and White-breasted Robins. And it's impossible to see too many of those three elusive south-western endemics.

The Southern Emu-wrens at Cheynes Beach are curious. They sit up on top of the bushes to investigate passers-by.

Noisy Scrubbird
White-breasted Robin
Red-eared Firetail
Southern Emu-wren

Cheynes Beach is as attractive as a postcard – and the birding's great too!

I found Red-eared Firetails hopping around the office at the Cheynes Beach caravan park.

Christmas Island

Today when Australians think of Christmas Island they think of the detention centre, asylum seekers and tragic drownings. Not so long ago, when Christmas Island was mentioned, the first thought was of the remarkable annual red crab migration, when millions of bright red crabs move from the mountains to the sea to spawn. For birders, Christmas Island will always be special. There are 11 species you can't see anywhere else in Australia, and so many vagrants that most birders manage a rarity when they visit.

The first time I visited Christmas Island, I ticked seven lifers as we drove from the airport to our lodgings: Christmas Imperial Pigeon, Christmas White-eye, Island Thrush, Red-footed Booby, Christmas Island Swiftlet (which at the time we called Glossy Swiftlet, then later Linchi Swiftlet), Christmas Frigatebird and Great Frigatebird. However, I missed two species on that trip. I had to go back to see the White-breasted Waterhen and the Christmas

White-tailed Tropicbirds lay their single egg on the ground at the base of a tree. The endearing chicks are quite unprotected.

The Christmas Imperial Pigeon is common and easily seen.

Island Thrush
Java Sparrow
Christmas White-eye
AND, IF YOU'RE VERY LUCKY
Savanna Nightjar

Boobook (which at the time we called Christmas Island Hawk-Owl). It's a long way to go for two ticks.

Located in the Indian Ocean, 312 kilometres south of Java and 1,400 kilometres north-west of Australia, Christmas Island is a little piece of Asia we like to call our own. It is 135 square kilometres and over 60 per cent of the island is national park. Planes often have trouble landing on Christmas Island due to the weather. A couple of times when I've flown there, we were delayed and concerned that we wouldn't be able to land.

A few years ago, Yellow Crazy Ants threatened to destroy the ecology of the island. Originally from either Malaysia or Singapore, the ants had been here for many years but for some reason, the population suddenly exploded and created supercolonies. The ants ate the crabs that ate seedlings, and encouraged scale insects that spread sooty mould and promoted weed invasion. A multi-million-dollar baiting program has reduced the number of ants significantly.

Christmas Island is uncomfortably hot and sticky. Apart from the red crabs, and huge robber crabs (the largest land invertebrates on earth!), I remember cool, inviting rainforests, frigatebirds swooping into the swimming pool at the abandoned casino, and adorable downy tropicbird chicks.

Most birders get Barn Swallows, Abbott's Boobies and introduced Java Sparrows. After my first visit, the Brown Goshawk on Christmas Island was granted species status (then called the Variable Goshawk), so I achieved an armchair tick. It really hurt later again when authorities decided it was, in fact, a race of the Brown Goshawk and I had to remove it from my lifelist. I eagerly await another change of mind, which seems to me to be inevitable one day.

Eight seabirds nest on Christmas Island – two can be found nowhere else: Abbott's Booby and Christmas Frigatebird. The White-tailed Tropicbird here has a yellow suffusion and is known locally as the Golden Bosunbird. The other five seabirds also nest on other Pacific and Indian Ocean tropical islands. They are Brown and Red-footed Booby, Great and Lesser Frigatebird and Red-tailed Tropicbird.

Christmas Island is a very special place. Birders sometimes return home without seeing the boobook, but I've never met a birder who wasn't enthusiastic about the place, and like me, secretly pleased to have an excuse to return.

This Brown Booby is unimpressed with the view from Margaret Knoll.

Phillip Island

Phillip Island has more to offer than Little Penguins and koalas – although, frankly, that's enough. It's great for both bush birds and waders and is one of the easiest places to see Cape Barren Geese. Rog and I had a holiday there in 1975 and I remember particularly admiring Restless Flycatchers in the cemetery and Hooded Plovers on the beach near Cape Woolamai. I remember, too, that everywhere we went we seemed to be accompanied by very friendly Grey Fantails. And I remember Little Penguins, dressed up in their dinner suits, crossing the roads dangerously at night.

Swan Lake on Phillip Island is good for waterfowl, appropriately mainly Black Swans.

Located in Western Port Bay, Phillip Island is just 90 minutes' drive from Melbourne. The island is about 20 kilometres long and about half as wide and is joined to the mainland by a bridge at San Remo. Here pelicans are fed daily at noon.

We usually drive directly to Observation Point at Rhyll, where we look down on a large expanse of tidal mudflats. Of course, you need a spotting scope to see the waders properly from the lookout. In summer we see Red and Great Knots, Bar-tailed Godwits and Eurasian Whimbrels. With their outlandish curved bills, colossal Far

*Short-tailed Shearwaters
are present on Phillip
Island from late
September until late April
each year.*

Little Penguin
Short-tailed Shearwater
Cape Barren Goose
Kelp Gull

Eastern Curlews look even bigger than they are (58 centimetres) beside tiny Red-necked Stints (15 centimetres). There are also Pacific Gulls and Greater Crested Terns on the mudflats, while beside us Brown Thornbills play in the mangroves with Silvereyes, and White-browed Scrubwrens scold noisily from the ground. Willie Wagtails chatter from the fence posts and gorgeous Eastern Rosellas fly overhead. Grey Shrikethrushes flute their melodious songs and Eastern Yellow Robins sit quietly looking intelligent with their black shining eyes. New Holland Honeyeaters are common, as are their White-eared relations.

Everyone goes to the Nobbies to admire the seals. From the boardwalk you can sometimes see Kelp Gulls (not common in Victoria) breeding on Seal Rocks.

On the road to the Nobbies there is a turnoff to Swan Lake, where there is a boardwalk which passes through a large Short-tailed Shearwater colony, leading to a couple of bird hides. These shearwaters are colloquially known as 'muttonbirds' because they look a little like Providence Petrels, which provided the staple diet for early settlers on Norfolk Island when crops failed and supplies did not arrive. Short-tailed Shearwaters are the most abundant Australian seabird, with a population of 23 million. About a million of these call Phillip Island home. They arrive with uncanny reliability on 25 September each year, locate a nesting burrow and a partner, raise a single chick, then leave in late April. They fly an impressive 8,000 kilometres to the Aleutian Islands in Alaska and thus enjoy two summers each year.

So you see, Phillip Island really does have much to offer besides koalas and Little Penguins.

*Little Penguins attract
millions of visitors to
Phillip Island every year.*

Terrick Terrick National Park

23

Terrick Terrick National Park – so good they named it twice. This park is situated between Mitiamo and Pyramid Hill in north central Victoria. Mitiamo is 222 kilometres north of Melbourne and 67 kilometres north of Bendigo; the park is 4 kilometres north of Mitiamo. It comprises one of the largest areas of unspoilt grasslands in Victoria, and is famous for being home to the now critically endangered Plains-wanderer. There are huge granite outcrops, lovely native woodlands and lots of wildflowers in spring.

Last time I was there it was winter. As I drove in, a large flock of White-winged Choughs flew through the native pines, giving their eerie whistles and incongruous rattles. Tree Martins chattered in the canopy, while a pair of Hooded Robins with their teenage son welcomed me to the picnic area. A Restless Flycatcher gave his guttural greeting and a Diamond Firetail pleaded for my attention. A Galah found a Yellow Box among all the native pines and noisily wiped his bill against the trunk, while his mate admired his efforts from above. A Wedge-tailed Eagle soared overhead, and Brown

Treecreepers flew from tree trunk to post and back again. A Striated Pardalote taunted me from the tippy-top of a gum tree. His call was loud and incessant, yet it took me several minutes to find him in my binoculars so I could add him to the day list.

As I set off on the short steep track to the summit of Mount Terrick Terrick, I disturbed a pair of Common Bronzewings. Australian Ringnecks and Red-rumped Parrots flashed past as I climbed, White-plumed Honeyeaters called out to encourage me and a Grey Shrikethrush hopped across the track in front of me. The view from the top of Mount Terrick Terrick made the climb worthwhile.

As I returned to the picnic area, I heard a Weebill. My time was limited, but I stopped to admire a Red-capped Robin and a small group of Southern Whiteface. Both Chestnut-rumped and Yellow Thornbills played in the native pines. A Little Eagle

Horsfield's Bronze Cuckoos migrate to Terrick Terrick National Park during the summer.

Jacky Winters are acrobatic, friendly and plentiful in Terrick Terrick National Park.

Last time I visited Terrick Terrick National Park, this Galah was noisily bill-swiping on a eucalypt. He had already removed quite a large area of bark.

circled overhead, looking at me curiously. Alarm calls filled the air and I assumed they were because of the Little Eagle. But then I saw a Brown Goshawk flying fast just below the top of the treeline. He was causing the consternation, not the Little Eagle, who seemed more interested in me than in finding a small bird for luncheon. As I drove out of the park, I lost count of the number of Jacky Winters on the fence posts. Let's just settle for lots.

This visit was very short, yet I had listed 25 species effortlessly. With such good winter birding, imagine how good it is when the summer migrants are present. There are Rainbow Bee-eaters, Rufous Whistlers, **Fairy Martins**, Painted Honeyeaters, Mistletoebirds and several species of cuckoo, the most common being Horsfield's Bronze Cuckoo.

In my experience, Terrick Terrick is **terrific** and well deserves the emphasis of repetition.

Painted Honeyeater (summer)
Jacky Winter
Hooded Robin
AND, IF YOU'RE REALLY LUCKY
Plains-wanderer

24

Daintree River cruise

I've done the Daintree River dawn cruise twice and I'm itching to do it again. Chris Dahlberg famously ran these tours for 18 years until Murray Hunt took over in 2011. Now they are called Daintree Boatman Wildlife Cruises.

Daintree is between Cairns and Cooktown in far north Queensland and is home to some exciting tropical birds. Every birder wants to see Great-billed Herons, Double-eyed Fig Parrots and Little Kingfishers. Great-billed Herons are rarely seen and most sought after. They inhabit inaccessible mangrove swamps and, despite their size (well over a metre), when they stand perfectly still by the water's edge they can be almost invisible.

Little Kingfishers are well-named – a tiny 12 centimetres of violet-blue jewellery. Considering that a House Sparrow is 15 centimetres from bill-tip to tail-tip, that's pretty small. We saw Little Kingfishers on both trips, along with their larger relations, Azure and Forest Kingfishers. Forest Kingfishers (which don't restrict themselves to forests) are beautiful birds that inhabit the tropics and subtropics. They are resident in the Daintree all year round.

On both trips we saw red-eyed Papuan Frogmouths, Spangled Drongos, Australasian Figbirds and Large-billed Gerygones. For a touch of colour, we had Green Orioles and Rufous Fantails. Brown Cuckoo-Doves sat silently watching us float by.

We saw lots of Eastern Cattle Egrets on both cruises. I still regard these as 'new' birds because they weren't around when I was growing up in Victoria, yet now they are common and widespread. The breeding birds show great character with their orange spiky hair and the young fledglings are about as ugly as sin.

The Forest Kingfisher does not restrict himself to forests and can be found in swamps, mangroves and along the Daintree River.

The first time we did the cruise was in spring and it poured with rain. The official trip report states that the weather was 'cool, calm, overcast, light rain'. Perhaps in the tropics they have a different definition of 'light rain'. All I know is that we were both soaked to the skin. We still saw 36 species of bird. The highlights were Topknot Pigeons, Scaly-breasted Lorikeets and a Channel-billed Cuckoo. We also saw Gould's Bronze Cuckoo, presently regarded as a bronze race of the Little Bronze Cuckoo. Metallic Starlings wheezed at us and Helmeted Friarbirds squawked.

The second cruise we did in winter, so we didn't see any cuckoos. The bonus was a Yellow-breasted Boatbill and both Spectacled and Pied Monarchs – and, it didn't rain. Whistling and Brahminy Kites flew overhead and Black-fronted Dotterels inspected the shore-line. And this time we saw a fourth Kingfisher   the Sacred, so called because Polynesians thought they had supernatural powers over the ocean. Australian Swiftlets that we had but glimpsed on our previous cruise, this time came close and dipped into the water for a drink as they flew past.

River cruises can be very relaxing (if it doesn't rain!) and a cruise on the Daintree, with the chance of seeing a Great-billed Heron, must be on every birder's to do list.

Great-billed Heron
Little Kingfisher
Double-eyed Fig Parrot
Papuan Frogmouth

25

Fogg Dam

Black-necked Storks wade through shallow blue water that is dotted with king-sized pink and white waterlilies – an interior decorator's dream. Comb-crested Jacanas promenade on the lily pads. Pairs of Green Pygmy Geese swim quietly among the lotuses, minding their own business. Fogg Dam is very picturesque.

Located 70 kilometres east of Darwin in the lower Adelaide River catchment, Fogg Dam is accessed via the Arnhem Highway. The best time to visit is between late March and early October. I recommend the Woodlands to Waterlily Walk that takes you into the wetlands on a boardwalk. It's easy walking, so you can allow yourself to be distracted by the birds. It is 2.2 kilometres and takes 45 minutes.

I've been to Fogg Dam three times and it just keeps getting better. The first time we visited, we were immediately impressed with the sheer number of

Black-necked Storks look majestic as they stride through the water. You can tell this one is a male by his black eye. The female's eye is yellow.

There is always a good variety of waterbirds at Fogg Dam.

Magpie Geese. Then we noticed the Green Pygmy Geese, Comb-crested Jacanas and Radjah Shelducks. Blue-winged Kookaburras squawked and screeched, Willie Wagtails chattered and Magpie-larks wandered around, indifferent to the cacophony.

The second time we visited, we saw Grey Whistlers, Azure and Forest Kingfishers, Varied Trillers and a Pheasant Coucal. Crimson Finches were common, as were Golden-headed Cisticolas. Sadly, we did not see any of their Zitting cousins, which are on the Fogg Dam bird list, but which are not seen often.

The third time we visited, we saw Pied Herons (lots of them), Brolgas and Glossy Ibis. Tawny Grassbirds flitted in the reeds and a single Nankeen Night Heron defied his moniker and looked very awake in the sunshine. There were darters, Wandering Whistling Ducks, an Australian Reed Warbler and Australasian Swamphen. We saw Whistling Kites and Intermediate and Great Egrets. We almost didn't notice our familiar friends Fairy Martins, Pied Stilts, Masked Lapwings, Royal Spoonbills, and Australian White and Straw-necked Ibis.

Although this is a dam and waterbirds predominate, I enjoyed the bush birds just as much. We saw Lemon-bellied Flyrobins, Peaceful and Bar-shouldered Doves, Paperbark Flycatchers and Green Orioles. Rainbow Bee-eaters entertained us with aerial displays, Red-tailed Black Cockatoos wailed overhead and Rufous-banded Honeyeaters played in the foliage above. There are 15 honeyeaters on the bird list, including White-gaped, White-throated and Bar-breasted. You can also see Rainbow Pitta and Rose-crowned Fruit Doves if you're lucky. There are Broad-billed Flycatchers and Large-billed Gerygones.

I thought it was all very beautiful and it couldn't get any better. Then, a White-browed Crake sauntered towards us, as friendly as you like. Howzat?

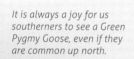

It is always a joy for us southerners to see a Green Pygmy Goose, even if they are common up north.

Black-necked Stork
Comb-crested Jacana
Green Pygmy Goose
Magpie Goose

Ken Haines

Gluepot Reserve

Gluepot Reserve has been a Mecca for twitchers since the property was purchased in 1997 by Birds Australia (now BirdLife Australia). Even before Scarlet-chested Parrots were discovered nesting here in 2011, the reserve was a must-do on every serious birdwatcher's itinerary. Birders hope to see endangered Black-eared Miners and the vulnerable eastern race of Regent Parrots, vulnerable Red-lored Whistlers and stately, vulnerable Malleefowl, as well as the most elusive and endangered Striated Grasswren.

Gluepot Reserve is situated in remote, hot, South Australia. It is one and a half hours' drive north of Waikerie on a good dirt road – well worth the effort, with a possible 190 bird species awaiting. There is an entry fee and the only accommodation is camping.

The reserve comprises 50,000 hectares of mallee scrub. It is dry woodland with casuarinas, sugarwood, bluebush and prickly spinifex.

My last visit was in winter 2012. We stopped to admire Southern Scrub Robins and Chestnut Quail-thrush just outside Gluepot. Crested Bellbirds called constantly – there must be a healthy population here. Striped Honeyeaters drew attention to themselves above our heads and Chestnut-crowned Babblers hopped through the undergrowth, chirring with amusement to see so many birdy-nerdies with binoculars so intent on ogling them.

As soon as we reached Gluepot, Gilbert's Whistlers greeted us. Then Striated Grasswren put on a spectacular injured mouse display right at our feet – too close for binoculars.

There are an impressive 17 honeyeaters on the Gluepot list – without a doubt, the most sought after being the Black-eared Miner. Birdwatchers must beware: Yellow-throated Miners are present too. At least they have the decency to display white rumps. The difficulty is that most flocks comprise not only Yellow-throated and Black-eared Miners, but also a good proportion of hybrids. The Black-eared Miners are much darker overall, with no white on the rump or tail. Naturally, the birds are highly mobile and don't pause to allow a birder to inspect their throat and facial markings. Some authorities assert that it is impossible to identify Black-eared Miners in the field and birders must be content to say that they've seen hybrids.

Perhaps the most common honeyeater is the Yellow-plumed, but there are also plenty of White-fronted, Brown-headed, Spiny-

The Scarlet-chested is arguably our most gorgeous parrot. These birds are curious and come to investigate birdwatchers.

26

Most so-called Black-eared Miners seen today are in fact hybrids. Look for a dark chin and a dark rump to identify the real thing.

Gluepot Reserve is 50,000 hectares of hot mallee scrub.

Scarlet-chested Parrot
Striated Grasswren
Regent Parrot (race *monarchoides*)
AND, IF YOU'RE VERY LUCKY
Black-eared Miner (but beware of hybrids)

cheeked, White-eared and those big bullies, Red Wattlebirds.

We had great sightings of White-browed Treecreepers, but Brown are also present, so careful identification is required. The White-browed has bolder belly striations and an appropriately thicker white eyebrow.

We were serenaded by Grey Butcherbirds (what a heavenly song!) and saw several Hooded and Red-capped Robins. Jacky Winters perched on tree trunks and waggled their tails at us. We didn't mind. We'd seen Gluepot at its best. It wasn't too hot and the birds were abundant and cooperative.

Picture postcard perfect, Chilli Beach is a good spot for Pacific Reef Heron and Brahminy Kites.

27 Iron Range National Park

Twitchers must go to Iron Range National Park to see Eclectus Parrots, Red-cheeked Parrots and Green-backed Honeyeaters. These birds are found nowhere else. There are lots of other great birds at Iron Range, such as entertaining Palm Cockatoos, tiny Yellow-billed Kingfishers, gorgeous Yellow-breasted Boatbills and stunning Black Butcherbirds.

On the far north-east coast of Cape York, Iron Range National Park, or Kutini-Payamu as it is now known, comprises 34,600 hectares of spectacular rainforest, open eucalypt forest and endless empty beaches. The best time to visit is between June and September, as access can be impossible during the wet.

We flew in from Cairns and easily saw both Eclectus Parrots and Green-backed Honeyeaters almost immediately. We also saw the northern race of the Australian Brushturkey with a purple neck collar, and Double-eyed Fig Parrots with red on the males' faces. Wompoo Fruit Doves greeted us with their weird vocalizations and Tropical Scrubwrens gleaned insects from low branches and vines. Meanwhile, Fairy and Large-billed Gerygones flitted in the foliage and Olive-backed Sunbirds and Mistletoebirds put on a colourful display.

Late in the afternoon, we sat by a dam watching honeyeaters come in for a drink. There were Tawny-breasted, Yellow-spotted, Varied and White-throated, and Dusky Myzomelas. There were red and green flowering melaleucas and red and white flowering eucalypts.

The next morning, chunky Red-cheeked Parrots flew overhead as we set off looking for Palm Cockatoos. We watched a Trumpet Manucode disgorge a red berry and admired a White-eared Monarch. Patience was required to obtain satisfactory sightings of a Northern Scrub Robin. To make up for this hard work, a Chestnut-breasted Cuckoo sat quietly while we drank him in, and, eventually, we had great views of those clowns of the bird world – Palm Cockatoos. The Magnificent Riflebird is aptly named – his iridescent blue-green breast plate has to be seen to be believed. The Red-browed Finches here are much brighter than the southern ones I know.

We found a pretty dam sprinkled with blue and white water lilies and looked for Spotted Whistling Ducks. All we saw were Green Pygmy Geese.

Ken Haines

The northern race of Australian Brushturkey has a purple collar. Southern birds have yellow collars. This bird seems to want two bob each way!

The Yellow-breasted Boatbill is a colourful little bird with a very large bill.

At Chilli Beach, we watched a dark phase Pacific Reef Heron flying low over the water and harassing the fish. In turn, a Brahminy Kite had a go at the egret.

That night we went spotlighting for frogmouths and saw red-eyed Papuan and orange-eyed Marbled, and a large green python. When we drove home, a Large-tailed Nightjar was sitting on our driveway to welcome us back.

Iron Range is a most welcoming place and the birding is, like the riflebird, magnificent.

Eclectus Parrot (now known as Moluccan Eclectus)
Red-cheeked Parrot
Green-backed Honeyeater
Australian Brushturkey
(race *purpureicollis* with a purple collar)

28

Gipsy Point

When I think of Gipsy Point, I think of Glossy Black Cockatoos, Black Bitterns and Azure Kingfishers. I remember Nankeen Night Herons, White-headed Pigeons and Red-browed Treecreepers. I picture gorgeous Australian King Parrots sitting in the morning sunshine and magnificent White-bellied Sea Eagles soaring overhead. I can hear the endless monotonous coo of the Wonga Pigeon, and the chauvinistic whip crack of the male Eastern Whipbird, answered immediately, obediently, by the quiet submissive 'chou chou' of the female.

Whenever I visit Gipsy Point, I take blue treasures and drop them conspicuously where a male Satin Bowerbird will be bound to spot them. It's a thrill to see my gifts appreciated and arranged carefully in his bower, issuing an irresistible invitation to any passing female.

Gipsy Point is six hours' drive from Melbourne – far enough from civilisation to leave the cacophony of city life behind. Located at the junction of the Genoa and Wallagaraugh Rivers at the head of Mallacoota

Inlet, Gipsy Point is synonymous with tranquillity and serenity. Pelicans and swans float by and fairywrens and finches hop around your feet. The world is at peace and all urgency is forgotten. The abundant kangaroos are unfazed by human presence and the furry swamp rats are cute and friendly. Fish jump out of the water with the sheer exuberance of simply being at Gipsy Point.

Gipsy Point is a good place for Grey Goshawks – they are not grey here but immaculate white. It used to be a great spot for Southern Emu-wren, but I haven't seen them here for some years. It remains a reliable location for Brown Gerygones – pretty little birds often overlooked as just one of the LBJs (little brown jobs).

The birding is always good but is at its best in summer, or, more accurately, from November to January, when the chances of seeing Glossy Black Cockatoos are best. With the typical capricious incongruity of bird nomenclature, glossy blacks are neither glossy nor truly black. They are dull brownish-black with bright red tail feathers. Females have variable yellow splotches on their heads. Glossies have a humorously large bill and bright, intelligent, shiny eyes. They are often seen in groups of three – that's mum, dad and this year's youngster – feeding quietly in casuarinas, working their way methodically from cone to cone.

We take Rainbow Lorikeets for granted because they are so common, but they really are very beautiful, very colourful birds.

Glossy Black Cockatoos are not glossy black at all, rather brownish black, but it's always a thrill to see them.

Youngsters often need help in cracking the tough cones – apparently it's quite a skill. There are three races of Glossy Black Cockatoos. Subspecies on the central Queensland coast and on Kangaroo Island are sedentary. The population that visits Gipsy Point breeds in New South Wales or Queensland in autumn and winter, then travels south to enjoy Victorian casuarina cones in summer.

I saw my first glossies at Gipsy Point and it is one of my fondest memories. Australian King Parrots might be more colourful, and Black Bitterns might be rarer, but for me the glossy blacks epitomise Gipsy Point.

Always peaceful and serene, Gipsy Point might just be the birdwatcher's perfect getaway.

Glossy Black Cockatoo
Azure Kingfisher
Eastern Whipbird
AND, IF YOU'RE VERY LUCKY
Black Bittern

29

Parry Lagoons

In the far north of Western Australia, hot and dusty Wyndham does not leap to mind as the most desirable holiday destination. However, just south of Wyndham is a little bit of birdy heaven. It is a picturesque freshwater lake covered in water lilies and waterbirds, known as Parry Lagoons. The water is so clear you can see the catfish and the barramundi swimming around – as well as the freshwater crocodiles. The catfish probably explain the presence of White-bellied Sea Eagles. Just imagine a sheet of blue water,

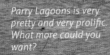

Parry Lagoons is very pretty and very prolific. What more could you want?

Brian Johnston

This Little Egret's yellow feet tell you it belongs to the Asian race.

with shimmering reflections of adjacent vegetation, dotted with green water lilies with huge pink and white flowers, and generously populated with Magpie Geese and Pied Herons. In the background, Brolgas and Black-necked Storks wade slowly through the water, pausing every so often when they spy some tasty morsel.

There were so many birds, we didn't know where to look first. We weren't there very long, but managed to clock up 35 species. We saw Green Pygmy Geese, Pacific Black Ducks, Radjah Shelducks and both common whistling ducks. With so many water lilies come Comb-crested Jacanas, quietly going about their business stepping from lily pad to lily pad. Australasian Grebes generally ignored us, but dived under the water if we got too close. We saw Australasian Darters, Glossy Ibis and Royal Spoonbills. There were Australasian Swamphens and four sorts of egret (Great, Intermediate, Eastern Cattle and Little) and White-faced, White-

necked as well as Pied Herons. The only cormorant we saw was a Little Pied. There were waders – Pied Stilts, Black-fronted Dotterels, Common Greenshanks and Masked Lapwings. There were even pelicans.

But perhaps the most interesting birds weren't waterbirds at all, they were Star Finches. Several of them, hopping around happily, allowing us to get quite close. There were also Chestnut-breasted Mannikins and Golden-headed Cisticolas. Those playful clowns, Grey-crowned Babblers were yahooing around the place and gorgeous Rainbow Bee-eaters hawked for insects over the water. The only raptors we saw (apart from the sea eagle) were, appropriately, a Swamp Harrier, and, synonymous with northern Australia, Black Kites. And I mustn't overlook the Torresian Crow.

The most surprising omission from our list was the Magpie-lark. Nor did we see Black Swans or Pink- eared Ducks or Hardheads. There are 11 honeyeaters on the Parry Lagoons bird list, but we didn't see any. The most common are Rufous-throated and White-gaped. Parry Lagoons is one of Australia's prettiest lakes, and certainly one of our most prolific.

Unlike its Queensland cousins, the Western Australian race of the Star Finch is not endangered.

Brolga
Rufous-throated Honeyeater
Pied Heron
Star Finch

30

Mallacoota

Mallacoota has the advantage of beautiful bush birds, wonderful waterbirds, significant seabirds and showy shorebirds. Located on the far eastern tip of Victoria, Mallacoota sometimes attracts rare waders, such as the White Wagtail that turned up in 2005. What more could a birder want?

In the first edition of this book, I placed Mallacoota in the top ten sites, however, much of Mallacoota was destroyed in the devastating 2019 bushfires, so it must be temporarily downgraded.

The bush is regenerating, all the wonderful walks have reopened and birds are returning. However, the iconic bloodwoods have not flowered since the fires, so there is still some way to go before Mallacoota returns to its former birding glory.

Meanwhile, there is plenty to see.

Perhaps the best place to start is Captain Stevenson's Point. Here you really need a spotting scope. There will be waterbirds on the sand spits below and in summer there'll be waders, including Eurasian Whimbrels and Far Eastern Curlews. There are always cormorants, teal, oystercatchers

Hooded Plovers can usually be seen on Betka Beach.

Great Egrets are very common at Mallacoota – and very elegant.

and Great Egrets. And while you're busy searching the water below, Silvereyes, Grey Fantails and honeyeaters will flit overhead.

There's an information booth on the wharf where you can pick up a brochure describing all Mallacoota's marvellous walks. I do Casuarina Walk (looking for bush birds) and Heathland Walk (hoping for Eastern Ground Parrots). If there's time, I'll include Pittosporum Walk, which goes from the caravan park to the beach. I've seen Painted Buttonquail here as well as Black-faced Monarchs.

A little out of town, on the road back to Genoa, Double Creek Nature Trail takes just 20 minutes. There are sometimes koalas snoozing in the gum trees and, if you're lucky, lyrebirds, distracted with their scratching, sometimes allow you to approach quite close.

It's worth driving to the airport to look for robins. You could see Rose, Pink, Scarlet or Flame. There may well be Tawny-crowned Honeyeaters and Jacky Winters. Latham's Snipe have been seen at the small pond here in summer. And you can be sure of contented kangaroos.

I always check out Betka Beach for Hooded Plovers. There are just 400 of these rare little birds in Victoria, and they nest in the sand dunes above the high tide mark. New signage insists that dogs are kept on a leash to protect the Hooded Plovers. Some dog owners respect the signs.

At Bastion Point in summer I watch Sanderlings running in and out with the waves on the beach, quite unfazed by nearby surfers.

Some Bar-tailed Godwits overwinter in Mallacoota, instead of returning to breed in Alaska as they should. They seem quite at home wandering around the grassy caravan park. Don't they know they're supposed to be on the beach?

Mallacoota is still a birdwatcher's heaven, fires notwithstanding. But, heed my advice: don't visit during school holidays.

Hooded Plover
Glossy Black Cockatoo
Wonga Pigeon
AND, IF YOU'RE VERY LUCKY
Eastern Ground Parrot

31 You Yangs Regional Park

Ask any Melbourne birder where to see a Tawny Frogmouth and, chances are, they'll say near the Park Office at the You Yangs. A pair has roosted there regularly for several years. And very beautiful they are too. This is also one of the most reliable spots around Melbourne to see elusive, critically endangered Swift Parrots.

The You Yangs Regional Park is 55 kilometres south-west of Melbourne, off the Geelong Road via the township of Little River. The park features dry eucalypt woodland with lots of large granite boulders. The bird list includes most of my favourite dry country birds, and thanks to a few small dams there are waterbirds too. In spring and summer, the

In autumn and winter, when the eucalypts are flowering prolifically, Swift Parrots can sometimes be seen at the You Yangs.

wildflowers are most attractive, and include several different orchids. The park is open daily from 8 am and is very popular with mountain bikers.

As well as Tawny Frogmouths near the Park Office you can see Superb Fairywrens, Red-browed Finches, Silvereyes and Willie Wagtails. Restless Flycatchers chatter happily from the canopy and lorikeets fly overhead, identifying themselves by the pitch of their screech. The most common is Purple-crowned, followed by Musk. You can also see Eastern and Crimson Rosellas and Red-rumped Parrots.

In summer there are Rufous Whistlers, Satin Flycatchers, Sacred Kingfishers and Rainbow Bee-eaters. In spring, watch out for Black-eared Cuckoos. In winter, if the eucalypts were flowering profusely there used to be a good chance of Swifts Parrots. You might still see one today if you are lucky. These birds breed in Tasmania in summer and spend winter on the mainland. However, the total population is estimated to be between 300 and 1,000 birds and is decreasing.

Tawny Frogmouths are seen regularly near the Park Office at the You Yangs.

Other good birding spots include Gravel Pit Tor and Eastern Flat. Here you can see Diamond Firetails, Crested Shriketits and Varied Sittellas.

Pied Stilts pose with the You Yangs as a backdrop.

I doubt it is possible to visit the You Yangs without seeing New Holland and White-plumed Honeyeaters and Red Wattlebirds. Altogether there are 15 honeyeaters on the bird list, including such sought-after species as Painted and Black-chinned. You'll see appealing little Eastern Spinebills, as well as two of my favourites, Brown-headed and White-eared.

Other birds hard to miss are Galahs, Sulphur-crested Cockatoos, Australian Magpies, White-winged Choughs and Welcome Swallows. Colourful Spotted Pardalotes are common, as are those little jewels, Mistletoebirds. You will certainly see Grey Shrikethrushes. Then there are some very special birds that are rarely seen, such as Speckled Warblers and Painted Buttonquail.

There are eight robins on the bird list, although I am told that Hooded Robins that used to be reliable, are no longer seen. The most common are Eastern Yellow, Jacky Winter, Scarlet and Flame. Red-capped, Rose and Pink are seen less frequently.

In summary, the You Yangs is a pleasant place for a summer picnic, mosquitoes and bull ants notwithstanding. The birding is good at any time of year, and in winter, there's always the breath-taking chance of seeing a Swift Parrot.

Tawny Frogmouth
Swift Parrot (autumn, winter)
Yellow-tufted Honeyeater
Crested Shriketit

32

Plumed Whistling Ducks outnumber their Wandering cousins at Hasties Swamp.

Hasties Swamp

Hasties Swamp is four kilometres south of Atherton in far north Queensland. (Atherton is about 90 kilometres south-west of Cairns.) Last time I was there, I was delighted to see that there is now a large bird hide. There's no need to go any further than that.

For me, the name Hasties Swamp is synonymous with Plumed Whistling Ducks. They are abundant. Every dead tree and every strip of muddy bank is packed wingtip to wingtip with Plumed Whistling Ducks. They can be noisy too. If they all decide to whistle at once, you'll need to cover your ears.

Other abundant birds at Hasties Swamp are Magpie Geese, Pacific Black Ducks, Australasian Swamphens and Eurasian Coots. You'll see lots of

Hasties Swamp is home to thousands of Whistling Ducks.

Wandering Whistling Ducks too, sprinkled among their plumed cousins. And herons and egrets and ibis and other waterfowl.

And now for the good birds. Sarus Cranes are common. (Extraordinary to think Sarus Cranes that look quite similar to Brolgas weren't discovered in Australia until 1966. Well done, Fred Smith.) Forest Kingfishers and Chestnut-breasted Mannikins are common too. So are Comb-crested Jacanas and Rufous Shrikethrushes (that we used to call Little Shrikethrushes.). Lewin's Rails, and Green and Cotton Pygmy Geese are not.

You could happen across any of those wonderful

Lewin's and Yellow-faced – they're very common.

Charming little Red-backed Fairywrens hop among the undergrowth and Mountain Thornbills tease you, hiding in the foliage. I often think that some birds get a great deal of fun at the birdwatcher's expense.

There are some good cuckoos on the list. There are Oriental and Channel-billed Cuckoos, as well as Brush, Fan-tailed and Shining Bronze. Ungainly Pheasant Coucals dash through the undergrowth and Australian Painted-snipe lurk among the reeds. There could be Topknot Pigeons and Brown Cuckoo-Doves. For a touch of colour, you might see

Sarus Cranes are often in mixed flocks with Brolgas. The Sarus Cranes have more red on their heads and necks.

Plumed Whistling Duck
Sarus Crane
Forest Kingfisher
Chestnut-breasted Mannikin

north Queensland birds like Olive-backed Sunbird, Bower's Shrikethrush, Chowchilla or even a Fernwren. You might see a Blue-billed Duck or a Glossy Ibis. And Pacific Baza, Square-tailed Kite or Grey Goshawk could possibly put in an appearance.

There are 16 honeyeaters on the Hasties Swamp list, and these include Macleay's, Bridled and Yellow – all easily identified. Graceful and Yellow-spotted Honeyeaters are put here, I'm sure, just to cause arguments about identification. You'll certainly see

Scaly-breasted Lorikeets or Pale-headed Rosellas.

There might well be White-browed or Spotless Crakes, and there could be Pacific Golden Plovers and Latham's Snipe. Bush Stone-curlews might stand cryptically under a tree, quite invisible until they move. There are four sandpipers on the list: Common, Marsh, Sharp-tailed and Wood.

So you see, there's quite a smorgasbord to choose from. Take your lunch and sit in the hide for a while. I guarantee you won't be disappointed.

33

Mareeba Tropical Savanna and Wetland Reserve

Years ago, I was put off visiting the Mareeba wetlands by the publicity. Advertisements featuring David Bellamy encouraged families to have a fun day out and enjoy canoeing on the wetlands. Among all that family fun, I couldn't see that there'd be much opportunity for good birding. How wrong I was.

The reserve is run by a non-profit community organization. It is 14 kilometres from the Mareeba township, which is about an hour's drive west of Cairns. The reserve is 2,000 hectares, comprising wetlands and savanna grasslands. Hence the bird list features both Brolga and buttonquail. There are certainly Painted Buttonquail, and there are reports of Buff-breasted, which I don't think anyone believes any more. I would have thought that Red-backed or Red-chested were more likely.

When I first came here, they were breeding Gouldian Finches in an attempt to replace the previously healthy but now extinct local population.

You'll see lots of waterbirds at Mareeba Wetlands.

At that time Gouldian Finches were classified as endangered. The bad news is that it didn't work. The released birds did not survive. They probably became lunch for a hungry Whistling Kite or a tasty snack for a Wedge-tailed Eagle. The good news is that Gouldian Finches are no longer endangered. While you won't see one at Mareeba, the population elsewhere is increasing and the endangered classification has been removed.

While you may not see Gouldian Finches at Mareeba, you will see Double-barred and Black-throated Finches and probably Chestnut-breasted Mannikins. There are lots of other good birds you will see. Both Forest Kingfishers and Blue-winged Kookaburras are common. Squatter Pigeons are common too. Here it is the northern race with a red eye-ring. Both Peaceful and Bar-shouldered Doves are common, as are Bush Stone-curlews.

You will certainly see Comb-crested Jacanas and Green Pygmy Geese, Little Pied Cormorants, Welcome Swallows and Blue-faced Honeyeaters.

Of course there are lots of waterbirds – lots of species and lots of birds. There are Sarus Cranes as well as Brolgas. There are Black-necked Storks, cormorants and coots, ducks and darters. There are pelicans, swans, Magpie Geese, ibis and egrets. There are sea eagles, ospreys and crakes.

Here you can see Australia's largest bird, the Emu, alongside the smallest, the Weebill. You can see Brown Quail and Golden-headed Cisticolas. There are Pied Butcherbirds, Willie Wagtails and Rainbow Bee-eaters. There are whistlers and waders, drongos and dollarbirds. There are nightbirds and honeyeaters, cuckoos and parrots. In fact, just about everything except Gouldian Finches.

Peaceful Doves can nest at any time of year, but do so more often from September until February.

You can tell that Bush Stone-curlews are nocturnal by their huge eyes.

Double-barred Finch
Black-throated Finch
Squatter Pigeon (race *peninsulae*)
Bush Stone-curlew

34

Tawny Grassbird
Horsfield's Bush Lark
AND, IF YOU'RE LUCKY
Asian Dowitcher
(summer)
King Quail

Knuckey Lagoon

Knuckey Lagoon doesn't look much – a small swamp, some water, some grassland. In fact, it looks like a bit of water lying around in a paddock, which, I suppose, is precisely what it is. But it can provide some very good birding.

It's about 12 kilometres south-east of central Darwin, off McMillans Road, and you enter on foot. A popular roosting site for Magpie Geese and Pied Heron, Knuckey Lagoon is home to Radjah Shelduck, Black-necked Stork and Comb-crested Jacana. King Quail live in the grass along with Tawny Grassbirds and Horsfield's Bush Larks. From September to December you can see waders: Little Curlew, Common, Sharp-tailed and Curlew Sandpiper. If you're lucky there could also be Asian Dowitcher, Long-toed Stint, Little Ringed Plover and Eastern Yellow Wagtail. There are four egrets here: Great, Intermediate, Eastern Cattle and Little, and White-necked Herons stride around the perimeter of the lagoon in a proprietary manner.

White-necked Herons prefer fresh water and are moderately common throughout most of the continent.

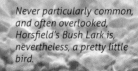

Never particularly common, and often overlooked, Horsfield's Bush Lark is, nevertheless, a pretty little bird.

Knuckey Lagoon boasts a diversity of waterfowl. The yellow eye informs us that this is a female Black-necked Stork.

Check the Gull-billed Terns to ensure they're not recently split Australian Terns. Whiskered Terns can also be seen and White-winged Terns appear from October to March.

I'm told you can see Swinhoe's Snipe at Knuckey Lagoon, but I have not witnessed them myself. The best time would be between November and January.

Garganey are also rumoured to be present, but I have heard that they have not been recorded in Darwin since the avian flu in 2004.

More likely are White-browed Crake and that much sought-after little bird, the Zitting Cisticola. However, birders beware: the very similar Golden-headed Cisticola is also present. There are Green Pygmy Geese and Wandering Whistling Duck, and Little Black and Little Pied Cormorants. Australasian Grebe swim among the lily pads and Australasian Darter sit on the shore with their wings in scarecrow pose. Straw-necked Ibis are more common than Australian White, and sometimes there are Glossies. Whistling and Black Kites are regulars, as are Masked Lapwings. You will see Magpie-larks and probably Australasian Figbirds. Both Tree and Fairy Martins visit Knuckey Lagoon and Paperbark Flycatchers are seen more often than not.

Willie Wagtails are not common, nor are Oriental Dollarbirds or Red-backed Fairywrens. But you might see Red-winged Parrots or Red-collared Lorikeets. You will probably see both Bar-shouldered and Peaceful Doves, and Sulphur-crested Cockatoos are possible, as are Little Corellas, Galahs and even Red-tailed Black Cockatoos.

Altogether, it is quite an impressive list.

So you might think it was an empty paddock with a bit of water, but Knuckey Lagoon could give you a pleasant surprise.

35

Waychinicup National Park

The first time we visited Waychinicup National Park we were struck immediately by the rugged coastal scenery. Then we noticed the extraordinarily large number of goannas. Located 45 minutes' drive east of Albany in the south-west of Western Australia, Waychinicup National Park comprises 6,310 hectares of woodlands and heathlands, and incorporates the lower reaches and the estuary of the Waychinicup River. It lies within the Two Peoples Bay and Mount Manypeaks Important Bird Area. Specifically, the important birds are the endangered Carnaby's Black Cockatoo, Noisy Scrubbird, Western Bristlebird and Black-throated Whipbird, and the critically endangered Western Ground Parrot. These are, of course, the main drawcards for birders. There are also other western specialties, such as Western Rosellas, Red-capped Parrots, Western Spinebills, Western Wattlebirds, Western Fieldwren, White-breasted Robins and Red-eared Firetails.

Then there are western races, such as the local race of Australian Ringnecks, known as Port Lincoln Parrots (distinguished from the Twenty-eight Parrot found nearer Perth).

The Grey Currawongs are a western race too, slightly darker than their eastern cousins. They are the only currawongs in Western Australia (making identification easy) and, unlike their Pied relations, are usually shy and wary. However, they are quick learners, and when exposed to people, soon grasp that picnic grounds mean free food. Luckily, they are not yet as aggressive as eastern Pied Currawongs. The White-cheeked Honeyeaters are also a western race, with a longer bill and a smaller white cheek. We watched them performing spectacular display flights, flying straight up into the air and certainly achieving their aim of drawing attention to themselves.

Believe it or not, some people visit Waychinicup for reasons other than birding, such as bush walking

Black-throated Whipbirds are more easily heard than seen.

or fishing or hang gliding. No accounting for taste.

Cheynes Beach nestles into the eastern boundary of Waychinicup National Park, and most of the species you find at Cheynes Beach, you also find at Waychinicup. In both places we saw Inland Thornbills, and Splendid and Red-winged Fairywrens. However, there are several birds on the Waychinicup list that don't feature at Cheynes Beach. These include Western Corellas, Rock Parrots, Yellow-plumed and White-naped Honeyeaters, Striated Pardalotes, Varied Sittellas, Gilbert's Whistlers and, surprisingly, a bird that I thought you'd see just about anywhere in Australia, the Magpie-lark.

Waychinicup has lots to offer – huge granite boulders, pristine empty beaches, dense coastal heath. The birds are a bonus.

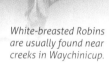

White-breasted Robins are usually found near creeks in Waychinicup.

Western Bristlebird
Red-winged Fairywren
Red-capped Parrot
AND, IF YOU'RE LUCKY
Black-throated Whipbird

Spectacular Scarlet Banksias (Banksia coccinea, sometimes called Waratah or Albany Banksia) are common at Waychinicup National Park.

36

Cape York

Rog and I first visited the tip of Cape York, the northernmost point of mainland Australia, in November 1994. We had great views of those hilarious clowns, Palm Cockatoos, went spotlighting for Papuan Frogmouths, and endured a long hot walk to the bower of the Fawn-breasted Bowerbird. Obligingly, the bird appeared almost immediately. We admired pretty Northern Scrub Robins and saw (and heard!) extraordinary Trumpet Manucodes. What a weird call these birds have – it doesn't sound anything like a trumpet blast to me. I describe it as halfway between the mating call of a bullfrog and the sound of someone vomiting violently. The name Manucode derives from Old Javanese *manok dewata*, meaning 'bird of the gods'.

Magnificent Riflebirds lived up to their name. We saw children's pythons, northern bandicoots and a cuscus eating poisonous seeds. Bravely, (or perhaps stupidly) I climbed a vertical 12-metre ladder leading to a tree hide and saw absolutely nothing. I climbed down again and saw Frilled Monarchs. One morning I walked to Evans Bay before breakfast and saw a White-tailed Tropicbird. We saw Metallic Starlings nesting in smooth-barked eucalypts that snakes could not navigate. I saw six species of honeyeater new to me and went home with 16 lifers and some bad sandfly bites. Instead of celebrating my lifers, I lamented the fact that I'd dipped on Ashy-bellied White-eyes and Yellow-billed Kingfishers.

In 1994 we stayed at Pajinka Wilderness Lodge, 400 metres from the tip of Cape York. We returned in 2006 (in order to reverse the white-eye and kingfisher deficiency) and this time we stayed in an air-conditioned motel in Bamaga, which is 33 kilometres further south. It was January and extremely hot and sticky with unpredictable occasional torrential rain. We visited what had

On the northern tip of Cape York, Metallic Starlings nest in colonies in smooth-barked eucalypts that snakes can't negotiate.

Red-bellied Pitta
Trumpet Manucode
White-faced Robin
Fawn-breasted Bowerbird

once been the Pajinka resort, since
reclaimed by the rainforest.

We had wonderful views of
Yellow-billed Kingfishers on the first
day. Then we had equally good views
of Red-bellied Pittas and Chestnut-
breasted Cuckoos, as well as one enormous
black-headed python. We took small boats
to Little Woody Island and saw Ashy-bellied
White-eyes. We flew to Boigu Island in Torres
Strait, which was even hotter than Bamaga.
Here I took a photo of New Guinea, four
kilometres away, and looking much closer.
We saw 47 bird species on Boigu, including
Collared Imperial Pigeons flying overhead.

We saw White-faced Robins and
Yellow-legged Flyrobins, and renewed
our acquaintanceship with all the lovely
honeyeaters we'd seen 14 years previously.
When we saw Black-backed Butcherbirds,
I heaved a sigh of relief. It was the last Cape
York endemic on my list.

*Metallic Starlings eat mostly
fruit, but also some insects.*

*Red-tailed Black
Cockatoos may be
common, but they're
always a joy to see. This
is a female.*

Eastern Bluebonnet
Budgerigar
Weebill
Zebra Finch

*True to its name, the
Nankeen Night-Heron feeds
at night. The striations show
this is a juvenile bird.*

37 Kinchega National Park

*White-plumed
Honeyeaters, sometimes
known as Greenies, have
a wide distribution across
the continent.*

Located 110 kilometres south-east of Broken Hill, Kinchega National Park is about as remote as you can get. It is 840 kilometres west of Sydney and you can sense every isolated kilometre. The park incorporates the Menindee Lakes system and the Darling River forms the eastern boundary. It is 443 square kilometres of river red gums, red earth and, in a good year, water. It used to be a pastoral property and the historic woolshed still stands – just.

Here you can find waterbirds and woodswallows, parrots and pigeons, honeyeaters and raptors.

After the ubiquitous Galahs and inquisitive Emus, the most common birds are Whistling Kites, Crested Pigeons, Peaceful Doves, Australian Magpies and, one of my favourites, White-plumed Honeyeaters. I grew up calling these birds 'Greenies'. Giving them a nickname somehow made them friends and I love to see them wherever I travel in Australia. They have regional accents that vary noticeably. My brother always says the Victorian birds say, 'Shit a brick!'

Next most common are Great Egrets, Nankeen Kestrels,

Laughing Kookaburras, Brown Treecreepers, Black-faced Cuckooshrikes, Australian Ravens and Welcome Swallows. Equally populous are the black and white brigade: Willie Wagtails, Magpie-larks, White-winged Choughs and Pied Butcherbirds.

You can see Silver Gulls here – such a long way from the sea. By contrast, you can see birds that like semi-arid conditions, like Chirruping Wedgebills, Crested Bellbirds and Zebra Finches.

There are seven parrots on the Kinchega list, ten honeyeaters and four woodswallows. The parrots include Bourke's Parrots and, predictably, budgies and bluebonnets. There are also colourful ringnecks and Mulga Parrots. The honeyeater list includes three chats and Little Friarbirds, as well as my childhood Greenies. The three honeyeaters

that vie with each other for claiming the most widespread distribution for an Australian honeyeater, Singing, Spiny-cheeked and Yellow-throated Miner, are all present in good numbers. White-fronted and Brown-headed are not so common. It seems to me that both Dusky and Little Woodswallows, which are not on the list, could very easily be seen here, in which case birders could experience a full hand of woodswallows.

When there's water about, there are swans, ducks, grebes and cormorants. There are pelicans and darters and ibis. You could even see a Nankeen Night Heron roosting in the river reds or stalking along the water's edge, quite content to be so far from civilization.

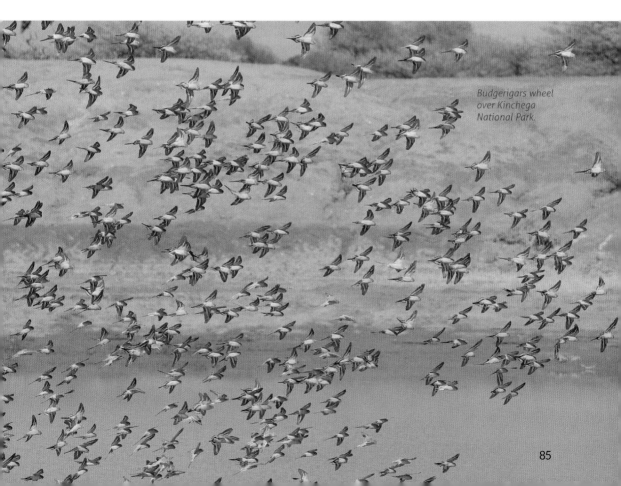

Budgerigars wheel over Kinchega National Park.

38

A handsome Far Eastern Curlew flies past.

Stockton Sandspit

Stockton Sandspit is the best site for waders in the Hunter Estuary. Many thousands of migratory shorebirds breed in the northern hemisphere in June and July, then fly 10,000 kilometres to make Stockton Sandspit their summer home. It is a phenomenal journey and these beautiful birds do it every year.

It is both the number of birds and the number of species that make this place special. There are sandpipers, godwits and greenshanks, stints, knots and plovers, tattlers, turnstones and curlews.

Even in winter the birding is good. Several non-migratory waders are resident all year round and breed when conditions are to their liking. These include Pied Oystercatchers, Pied Stilts, Red-capped Plovers, Black-fronted Dotterels and Masked Lapwings. And a few of the young migratory waders, not yet ready for breeding, overwinter too. These include Bar-tailed Godwits and Far Eastern Curlews.

Stockton is a suburb of Newcastle, north of the Hunter River. Newcastle is on the mid-north coast of New South Wales, 167 kilometres north of Sydney. The sandspit has been established by removal of mangroves and construction of a lagoon, giving the birds a direct view to the open water. To people other than birders or fishermen, the site underneath a busily trafficked bridge would not be in the least alluring. Birders know better. There is a bird hide (the key can be collected from the Fern Bay Store) and an informative sign, with good photos to help novice birders identify what they are seeing.

The waders feed on the exposed mudflats at low tide and roost on sandy beaches at high tide. Grey-tailed Tattlers prefer roosting on the oyster-encrusted rocks, where their grey plumage merges into the background and makes them very difficult to spot. You'd think that a Terek Sandpiper with its long upturned bill and distinctive orange legs would be quite conspicuous, but they, too, can be cryptic among the rocks. Even stunning Pacific Golden Plovers, which can be in breeding plumage when they

Bar-tailed Godwit
(summer)
Far Eastern Curlew
(summer)
Grey-tailed Tattler
(summer)
Pacific Golden
Plover (summer)

Thousands of migratory waders from the northern hemisphere visit the Stockton Sandspit every summer.

There are both Black-tailed Godwits (with straight bills) and Bar-tailed Godwits (with bills slightly upturned) here. Some have remnant breeding plumage.

arrive in September or just before they leave in April, can be hard to see. They stand perfectly still and their spectacularly speckled plumage disappears among the shadows, so it can take some effort to pick them out.

Red-necked Avocets are not so coy and there can be several thousands of them at Stockton Sandspit. With their pretty upturned bills, and beautiful bright chestnut heads and necks, they really are extremely elegant birds.

There's no doubt in my mind that it's worth a drive to Stockton at any time, but particularly in summer.

39

Comerong Island Nature Reserve

Comerong Island Nature Reserve is a top spot for migratory waders. The reserve is 660 hectares and comprises three different habitats: tidal mud flats, mangrove swamp and littoral forest. Accordingly, there are many waterbirds and bush birds as well as shorebirds.

Comerong Island is located in the delta of the Shoalhaven River, 15 kilometres east of Nowra, 50 kilometres south of Wollongong. You can often walk to Comerong Island from Shoalhaven Heads as the river entrance is regularly blocked by sand. To get to Shoalhaven Heads, take Bolong Road from Nowra. In the Shoalhaven Heads car park, there are some excellent information signs about the migratory waders. Alternatively, if you don't want to walk (or if the entrance isn't blocked), there is a vehicular ferry. In this case, from Nowra take Moss Street, then Terara Road. The ferry costs $11 return,

but was free last time we were here because the machine had broken down.

There are 90 waders on the Comerong Island bird list, including several summer migrants from the northern hemisphere protected by international agreements, notably Pacific Golden Plovers, Far Eastern Curlews and Eurasian Whimbrels. In winter you'll see Double-banded Plovers that have flown over from New Zealand. Almost half of the entire New South Wales population of these dear little birds is found on Comerong Island.

You'll also see Pied and Sooty Oystercatchers, Ruddy Turnstones, Bar-tailed Godwits, Common Greenshanks and Red-necked Stints. There are both

Scarlet Myzomela
White-fronted Chat
White-bellied Sea Eagle
Sooty Oystercatcher

A White-bellied Sea Eagle flies past Comerong Island.

Osprey and White-bellied Sea Eagles on the bird list. Comerong Island provides a refuge for several threatened species, including Blue-billed Ducks, Hooded Plovers, Great Knots, Black-tailed Godwits, and both Lesser and Greater Sand Plovers.

In winter, when temperatures drop in the mountains, thousands of swans and ducks flock to the warmer coastal waters of the Shoalhaven estuary. So do herons, egrets, ibis, cormorants and pelicans.

There are great birds in the forest too. It's always exciting to see a Scarlet Myzomela. There are also such prepossessing creatures as Spangled Drongos, Topknot Pigeons and Eastern Whipbirds. Comerong Island is the furthest south you'll see Bar-shouldered Doves and you can see Pacific Emerald Doves here also. Watch out for Sacred Kingfishers and Variegated Fairywrens.

I heartily recommend Comerong Island for all birders. In fact, the only negative thing I can think of to say about it is that I encountered ticks here – of the blood-sucking insect variety, not the preferred handwritten additions to my lifelist.

Far Eastern Curlews visit Comerong Island every summer.

Male Scarlet Myzomelas are brilliant birds, but they often feed high in the canopy and can be difficult to observe.

Fitzgerald River National Park is located on the coast, at the mouth of the Fitzgerald River.

40

Fitzgerald River National Park

Birders know Fitzgerald River National Park as the best place to see Black-throated Whipbirds, and a good place to look for Western Bristlebirds. As long as you don't have unrealistic expectations of actually seeing one, it is also somewhere to seek the elusive critically endangered Western Ground Parrot.

The park comprises 330,000 hectares of heathland, mallee and timbered gullies. Much of it is wilderness accessed only by foot. It is located 420 kilometres south-east of Perth on the central south coast of Western Australia, between the popular fishing townships of Bremer Bay and Hopetoun. Roads are closed when it is wet. Because of its botanical significance, it has been designated

a World Biosphere Reserve. Apart from the wildflowers (best in spring), people come to the Fitz for camping, fishing, bushwalking, whale watching (June to November) and, of course, the birds. There are around 210 species on the bird list.

Splendid Fairywrens, Purple-gaped Honeyeaters, Purple-crowned Lorikeets and Southern Scrub Robins are all common. So are Blue-breasted Fairywrens, Shy Heathwrens and Inland Thornbills. Tawny-crowned Honeyeaters and the yellow-rumped race of Spotted Pardalotes are easily seen. The local race of Australian Ringnecks, known as Port Lincoln Parrots, is unavoidable. That's not a bad list of desirable birds. And they're all common.

Moderately common species include Hoary-headed Grebe, Stubble Quail and Banded Lapwing. There are also Regent, Red-capped and Elegant Parrots. Then there are Shining Bronze Cuckoos, Spotted Nightjars and Southern Emu-wrens. As well as Western Spinebills, White-browed Babblers and Black-throated Whipbirds. Yes, I said Black-throated Whipbirds. Birders who've spent days listening to the tormenting call of this invisible bird at Two People's Bay or Cheynes Beach may find it difficult to believe, but Black-thrated Whipbirds are moderately common at Fitzgerald River National Park. More common than Western Yellow Robins or Western Gerygones or Western Fieldwrens.

There's a chance of Malleefowl and Square-tailed Kite, and both Carnaby's and Baudin's Black Cockatoos. Western Rosellas and Rock Parrots are on the list, along with Black-eared Cuckoos and Eastern Barn Owls. You might see Western Thornbills, Yellow-plumed Honeyeaters or Black-faced Woodswallows.

With ocean access, birds such as Little Penguin, Indian Yellow-nosed Albatross and Great-winged Petrel are on the bird list too. There are also lots of waders from the northern hemisphere, as well as beautiful Hooded Plovers, sadly now becoming as vulnerable in the west as they have been for many years in the eastern states.

After that, I'm afraid it's down to the rare birds. Birds like Australasian Bitterns, Baillon's Crakes and Gilbert's Whistlers. Or perhaps Ground Cuckooshrikes, Western Bristlebirds or Redthroats. And then there's the Western Ground Parrot.

Fitzgerald River National Park is a good place to see Western Yellow Robins.

Splendid Fairywren (race *splendens*)
Black-throated Whipbird
IF YOU'RE LUCKY
Western Bristlebird
AND, IF YOU'RE EXTREMELY LUCKY
Western Ground Parrot

It's always a thrill to see Hooded Plovers, which are becoming as rare in the west as they are in the eastern states.

41 Birdsville Track

Flock Bronzewings can still occur in large numbers along the Birdsville Track.

Cinnamon Quail-thrushes blend beautifully into the desert background.

The Birdsville Track traverses 517 kilometres from Marree in remote outback South Australia to Birdsville in south-west Queensland, and crosses both the Tirari and the Sturt Stony Desert, some of the harshest country Australia has to offer. Yet the birding is terrific.

This iconic track provides iconic birding. There are harsh stony plains just right for Gibberbirds and Cinnamon Quail-thrush. There are arid open deserts perfect for Australian Pratincole and Inland Dotterel, with an occasional bluebush for Banded Whiteface to sit up on. Eyrean Grasswren favour canegrass-covered sandhills, while Grey Grasswren prefer lignum surrounding swamps. Trees along the dry creekbeds provide roosts for Grey Falcon and Letter-winged Kites and any waterhole could accommodate flocks of budgies or Flock Bronzewings.

Nineteenth-century ornithologists wrote enthusiastically about immense clouds of Flock Bronzewings – hence the name. Birders today are excited to have a good view of a pair, but numbers occasionally irrupt. In 2011, it was estimated that there were 10,000 Flock Bronzewings at Mungeranie waterhole. What a sight that must have been! The largest flock I saw in 2012 was of about 100 birds.

Yellow Chats are seen sometimes at bore holes along the Birdsville Track and much more gorgeous Orange Chats are seen often. White-fronted Chats are not rare and this was the first place I saw male Crimson Chats with vivid episcopal cardinal breasts. I find that their breasts are usually a little blotchy. One large mixed flock of bright orange and crimson birds were little blobs of colour like Christmas baubles on each bush as far as I could see into the distance.

Lake Harry was full of water and full of waterbirds – unlike my first trip up the Birdsville Track, when it was as dry as Bill Bryson's humour. On this recent occasion, we saw Black Swans, Pink-eared and Maned Ducks, Grey Teal, Hardheads, Eurasian Coots, Australasian and Hoary-headed Grebes, Pied and Banded Stilts, and Masked and Banded Lapwings. Not a bad list for a desert, is it?

Driving into Mungeranie after dark, we saw Eastern Barn Owls and Southern Boobooks, as well as many long-haired rats, some pale grey, some quite black. So many rats exasperated all the unfortunate campers, but made us hope we might see a Letter-winged Kite. Alas, it was not to be.

I had to be satisfied with fantastic views of two Grey Falcons perched on a communication tower. One obligingly flew, showing himself to be distinctly elegant among the comparatively chunky Brown Falcons already in the air.

Every Australian birder must make the effort to travel the Birdsville Track. It is not too hot in winter, and if you happen to select a year when there's been some rain, the birding will be most rewarding.

Flock Bronzewing
Grey Grasswren
Eyrean Grasswren
AND, IF YOU'RE LUCKY
Grey Falcon

After a good season, the number of Budgerigars can increase enormously.

42

Green Cape
(Ben Boyd National Park)

Birders know Green Cape because of its Eastern Ground Parrots, and I agree that even a remote chance of seeing Eastern Ground Parrots is a pretty good reason for travelling somewhere. But there are lots of other good birds at Green Cape too.

Striated Fieldwrens, Beautiful Firetails and Crescent Honeyeaters are all common. If that's not enough, you can stand on the cliffs and watch albatrosses soar below. You can see Australasian Gannets out at sea plunge-diving into the water, or perhaps a shearwater, or a White-bellied Sea Eagle will fly by. Northern Giant Petrels are sometimes seen here, more often from May to October. These huge seabirds breed on Macquarie Island in summer, then explore the southern oceans when their chicks fledge. They are identified from Southern Giant Petrels by the colour of the bill tip: Northern have reddish-brown bill tips; Southern have pale green. That can be hard to do standing on a windy cliff-top.

Always more often heard than seen, Eastern Whipbirds are common. Even more common, Tawny-crowned Honeyeaters sit on top of a bush and regard you disdainfully as you intrude onto their territory. You'll probably find a Little Wattlebird feeding in a banksia. Where there are Eastern Ground Parrots, there are Southern Emu-wrens (although the reverse doesn't hold). Here there are also Superb Lyrebirds and Spotted Quail-thrush.

Ben Boyd National Park is in two distinct sections, north and south of Eden. Eden is a fishing town on Two People's Bay, about 500 kilometres south of Sydney. Green Cape is in the southern section of the park, via Edrom Road, 18 kilometres south of Eden. Habitats include heathland, woodland and rainforest.

In the rainforest, you might see Rufous Fantails, Eastern Yellow Robins, Brown Gerygones, Large-billed Scrubwrens and Bassian Thrushes. In the heathland, you could come across Chestnut-rumped Heathwren, White-browed Scrubwren and Brush Bronzewings. And in the open woodland, there's a good chance of Grey Fantail, Grey Shrikethrush, Pied Currawong and both Brown and Yellow-rumped Thornbills. Australian Golden Whistlers you could see anywhere.

Unlike their critically endangered western cousins, the Eastern Ground Parrots of eastern

Green Cape Lighthouse in Ben Boyd National Park, as seen from the sea.

The Northern Giant Petrel is identified by its reddish bill tip. The Southern Giant Petrel has a greenish bill tip.

mainland Australia are not imperilled. Their official classification is 'near threatened'. Without confidence the total population is estimated to be 6,700, of which only about 100 birds call Green Cape home. In my experience, these birds are never easy to see, but perhaps the easiest place is Barren Grounds. When I went looking for them at Green Cape in 1991, picking my way through the dense undergrowth with feigned confidence, I saw many more snakes than parrots. At Green Cape, you are more likely to see Australian King Parrots than Eastern Ground Parrots. But that's no reason not to look.

The Striated Fieldwren often sits high on a twig and gives his musical call.

Tawny-crowned Honeyeater
Eastern Spinebill
Striated Fieldwren
AND, IF YOU'RE LUCKY
Beautiful Firetail

43

Double-barred Finches always seem exceptionally neat and tidy to me.

Kununurra

Kununurra must be the finch capital of Australia. Birders go there to see Yellow-rumped Mannikins, but there are also Zebra, Double-barred, Long-tailed, Masked, Crimson, Star and Gouldian Finches, and Chestnut-breasted and Pictorella Mannikins. Last time I was there, there were Star Finches in a park right in the township! Double-barred and Crimson Finches are very common.

Kununurra is 3,040 kilometres from Perth in the far north-east of the Kimberley Region, quite close to the Northern Territory border. The town was established to service the Ord River Irrigation scheme and today the population is largely transient.

However, many birds are resident. Apart from finches, the most common birds are, in order, Peaceful Doves, Magpie-larks and Bar-shouldered Doves. Then come White-gaped Honeyeaters, Black Kites and Rainbow Bee-eaters. How exciting to have Rainbow Bee-eaters as one of your most common birds!

There are 16 honeyeaters on the Kununurra bird list and 15 raptors, including Black Falcon and Pacific Baza. Brown Honeyeaters are common, but there are also Grey and Grey-fronted, Banded and Black-chinned, as well as Silver-crowned Friarbirds.

Packsaddle Road is famous for finches – both Yellow-rumped and Chestnut-breasted Mannikins, and Star and Crimson Finches. We also saw Horsfield's Bush Lark and Spotted Harrier.

My most vivid memories of Kununurra are sitting beside a waterhole very early in the morning waiting for finches to come in for a drink. We sat uncomfortably for about an hour on rocks not designed as lounge chairs, trying hard to ignore the overwhelming stench of cattle. Galahs and Budgerigars sat in the trees watching us suspiciously. At last, at about 6 am, some Double-barreds allowed their thirst to conquer their fear of strangers. They were followed by a couple of zebbies, then about 100 Pictorella Mannikins with a very noisy flight. They were very nervous and flighty and breathtaking to watch.

Kununurra has White-quilled Rock Pigeons, Red-tailed Black Cockatoos and Paperbark Flycatchers. With lots of water, there are lots of waterbirds – ibis, herons, egrets, waders and ducks. I was intrigued by the noise made by the female Radjah Shelduck. It sounded like a slow hand-held drill. The male has an insignificant peep.

Add Blue-winged Kookaburras, Red-winged Parrots and White-breasted Woodswallows and you have quite a smorgasbord of birds. There's much to choose from, but it's hard to go past Kununurra's famous finches.

Lily Creek Lagoon, just one of Kununurra's good birding spots.

Yellow-rumped Mannikin
Double-barred Finch
Paperbark Flycatcher
Radjah Shelduck

You often hear the metallic 'prrrrt' call of the Rainbow Bee-eater before you see him.

Port Fairy pelagic

44

If you think that it's difficult identifying Graceful from Yellow-spotted Honeyeaters, or Brown from Tasmanian Thornbills or distinguishing between the corvids, you may be amused to consider the differences between Sooty and Short-tailed Shearwaters. The textbooks may tell you that Sooties are larger with narrow pointed wings and a narrow neck, while Short-tailed have rounded wings and rounded heads, but personally I cannot discern any difference.

Such are the joys of pelagic birding. You pay someone to give you a day's discomfort, perhaps with the added bonus of being seasick, and have a very slight chance of seeing something rare – which you may or may not be able to identify. No matter, there's always someone on board who knows what it is. Identification of seabirds is no longer the subject of lively debate it once used to be. Today there are always several large cameras recording the bird for posterity, giving plenty of unambiguous images and ruling discussion about identification redundant.

Recent pelagics I have experienced out of Port Fairy have been exceptionally civilized. Now there's a new big comfortable boat called *Southern Explorer* and it's licensed to carry 23 passengers. We are actually given morning tea! Delicious it is, too. This doesn't make it any easier to stand up and walk around the moving boat, but it certainly makes sitting still more comfortable.

Pelagics used to be run out of Portland, but not any more. The only regular Victorian pelagics now are out of Port Fairy. In the far south-west of Victoria, Port Fairy is 290 kilometres west of

Albatrosses squabble over berley on a Port Fairy pelagic.

The Black-browed Albatross wears attractive eye make-up and has more black on the underwing than most other white-bodied mollymawks.

Melbourne. The only downside is that the weather is often rough and trips are cancelled more often than they go. Consequently, I've never been out in winter.

On every Port Fairy pelagic I've done, I've seen Great-winged Petrels and Black-browed, Indian Yellow-nosed and Shy Albatross. We normally see Flesh-footed and Short-tailed Shearwaters, White-faced Storm Petrels and Buller's Albatross and we have been known to see all three jaegers (Parasitic, Pomarine and Long-tailed). In 2011 there was an irruption of Great Shearwaters, a bird previously classified as a vagrant; that is to say, there had been fewer than ten confirmed sightings of it. I was lucky enough to see one in April 2011 and again in February 2012. Perhaps my best sighting from this area was from Portland in February 1998, when a wonderful Sooty Albatross circled our boat.

Apart from that, one of the most breathtaking things I have ever seen anywhere, even if it wasn't a bird, was a blue whale, without a doubt the largest animal I've ever seen. We didn't measure it, but a female blue whale can grow to 33 metres and weigh 160 tonnes. That alone made the four-hour drive from Melbourne to Port Fairy worthwhile.

If you'd like to go on a Port Fairy pelagic, contact Neil Macumber at birdswing@bigpond.com.

Yellow-nosed Albatross
Great-winged Petrel
White-faced Storm Petrel
Parasitic Jaeger

Buller's Albatross is identified by the broad yellow line on the top of the bill.

The Little Friarbird has the largest range of all the friarbirds.

45 Cumberland Dam

The landscape around Georgetown in north Queensland is harsh. It's the sort of country where you expect to see Black Kites and Black-faced Woodswallows. The red earth is liberally scattered with termite mounds and straggly gidgee. Bustards and Brolgas stroll by looking quite at home. Twenty-four kilometres west of Georgetown, sitting incongruously in this austere terrain, lies Cumberland Dam, a little oasis in the wilderness.

White water lilies decorate the blue water, making it even more enticing. The barren red earth goes right to the water's edge; there is no softening margin of reeds or grasses to provide shelter for creatures coming in for a drink. Intermediate Egrets stride through the water looking for little fish and frogs. Comb-crested Jacanas step tentatively on the lily pads and Green Pygmy Geese and Hardheads swim safely in the middle of the dam.

Finches fly many miles to enjoy a drink here. In years gone by, this was a favourite spot for Gouldian Finches, but alas Gouldians are long gone from this part of the country. There are other finches though: Black-throated, Double-barred, Masked, Zebra and Plum-headed, as well as Pictorella and Chestnut-breasted Mannikins. The best time to see them is very early in the morning. Arrive before sunrise and sit quietly and wait.

Honeyeaters like this dam too. I photographed this Little Friarbird here in September 2000. There are Rufous-throated, Blue-faced, Yellow-tinted and Yellow. You'll also see Banded and Brown Honeyeaters, and Yellow-throated Miners.

Apostlebirds are common. I always like to count them to see if there really are a dozen in a group – that's why they're called Apostlebirds. Of course, there rarely are.

Every time I've visited Cumberland Dam, I've found a Great Bowerbird's bower. They are decorated predominantly with white treasures.

Great Bowerbirds are everywhere. These are our largest bowerbird, so it's appropriate to call them great. They collect white treasures as ornaments in their avenue bowers, and how they manage to protect them from wandering cattle, I do not know.

Birders go to Georgetown to see Squatter Pigeons and these pretty, pudgy pigeons can be seen at Cumberland Dam too. It is the northern race here with a red eye-ring. There are also Crested Pigeons and Peaceful Doves. Pied Butcherbirds flute their melodious songs and Black-faced Cuckooshrikes shuffle their wings uncertainly.

Mistletoebirds are here too, although I don't remember any mistletoe in the gidgee. There are large flocks of Budgerigars, raucous Blue-winged Kookaburras and colourful Red-winged Parrots. You can see both Restless and Paperbark Flycatchers, as well as Rufous Whistlers and Rainbow Bee-eaters.

Cumberland Dam really is a welcome oasis in the wilderness.

Masked Finch
Black-throated Finch
Mistletoebird
Pale-headed Rosella

Mistletoebirds are delightful little jewels, one of my favourites, with a very wide distribution across mainland Australia.

101

46

Barren Grounds Nature Reserve

The Barren Grounds Nature Reserve comprises over 2,000 hectares of heathland, woodland and rainforest, high on the Illawarra escarpment. It is 120 kilometres from Sydney, 200 kilometres from Canberra. The reserve was created in 1956 because it is home to two special birds: the Eastern Bristlebird and the Eastern Ground Parrot.

The once-endangered Eastern Bristlebird is easily seen at Barren Grounds.

Heyn de Kock

season. Scarlet Myzomelas are one of several interesting species of Australian birds where some populations are nomadic and some are sedentary. The Barren Grounds Scarlet Myzomelas are nomadic, flying north in summer and south in winter. My bird, in late March, was the vanguard of the southern movement.

We returned the next day and were successful, seeing several bristlebirds, as well as an antechinus. The bristlebirds were running across the track seemingly wherever we looked, making us wonder how we'd missed them the day before. We have seen bristlebirds most times we've visited, but they are not guaranteed, as our first failed visit attests.

I've never managed to see an Eastern Ground Parrot at Barren Grounds. They are currently classified as near threatened and the reserve is believed to accommodate half the New South Wales' population. Other birders assure me that it's easy to see them if you're at the right place at the right time!

The Barren Grounds bird list contains 180 species, which is not surprising given that there are

Barren Grounds comprises 2,000 hectares of heathland, woodland and rainforest.

Thanks to great conservation management, I'm delighted to report that the conservation status of the Eastern Bristlebird has been recently reclassified to near threatened.

On our first visit in March 2003, it was misty and hazy, and we did not see any Eastern Bristlebirds. I thought the dense vegetation was similar to that in the south-west of Western Australia, where we'd looked for Western Bristlebirds on many occasions.

I did see a Scarlet Myzomela, the first for the

four different habitats: the dense heathland suits Eastern Ground Parrots, Southern Emu-wrens and Beautiful Firetails; woodlands accommodate the bristlebirds; tall forest is where I saw the Scarlet Myzomela; and temperate rainforest is good for Olive Whistlers, Eastern Whipbirds, Bassian Thrushes, Pilotbirds and Superb Lyrebirds – or so the sign says. In my experience, the lyrebirds wander wherever they want. Crimson Rosellas, Yellow-tailed Black Cockatoos, Eastern Spinebills and black wallabies are all over the place too. Other good birds I've seen here include Speckled Warblers and Large-billed Scrubwrens.

In spring the flowers are gorgeous. There are waratahs, hakeas, peaflowers, boronias, heaths, orchids and insectivorous sundews. In winter, the large orange hairpin banksias are particularly striking and attract lots of honeyeaters. In November and December, the Christmas Bells are nothing short of spectacular.

Barren Grounds Nature Reserve is always worth a visit – even if it's too hazy for good views, or if you dip on Eastern Bristlebirds and Eastern Ground Parrots. Clearly, there's nothing barren about it.

Barren Grounds is probably the easiest place to see the Eastern Ground Parrot.

Eastern Bristlebird
Eastern Ground Parrot
Large-billed Scrubwren
Scarlet Myzomela

Singing Honeyeaters are found over most of the continent and will often respond to hand clapping.

47

Port Augusta

Port Augusta, the so-called 'Crossroads of Australia', is at the head of Spencer Gulf, 322 kilometres north of Adelaide. The Australian Arid Lands Botanic Garden in Port Augusta is probably the easiest and most reliable spot to see a Chirruping Wedgebill. As you wander around among the eremophila, you'll hear their distinctive chirrup before you see the neatly coiffed brown bird perched on top of a bush. This chirrup is the only feature that distinguishes him from his close relation, the Chiming Wedgebill, who, needless to say, chimes instead of chirruping. With their fetching stylish crests, they look like the delinquents of the bird world.

The most common bird in the garden is the Singing Honeyeater, followed by the Crested Pigeon, then the Spiny-cheeked Honeyeater. Other common birds include White-browed Babblers, Nankeen Kestrels and White-winged Fairywrens. Sit quietly at one of the bird hides and you may be rewarded with Zebra Finches coming in for a drink. Perhaps you'll see a Southern Whiteface or a Black-faced Woodswallow. Maybe a Hooded Robin will sit quietly nearby, or a Red-capped Robin may imitate a ringing telephone. In summer, when the grevilleas and eremophilas are overloaded with nectar, I've seen both Pied and Black Honeyeaters here.

Early one morning, I arrived at the garden before the gates were open. I could see a Redthroat on the other side of the fence, so I climbed over to take his photo. No sooner had I got him in focus, than the gardener arrived to unlock the gates. There was nowhere to hide. I figured I'd get an embarrassing dressing-down. The man approached and I attempted to smile benignly. He grinned.

'Did you get it?' he asked enthusiastically.

Clearly a good photo of a Redthroat was more important than deference to restrictive opening hours. Just then a Grey Butcherbird performed his melodious song, blessing my naughtiness and the gardener's good will. I felt vindicated.

Apart from being a reliable spot for Chirruping Wedgebills, Port Augusta can be a good place for Banded Stilts. There is often a large flock huddled together in Spencer Gulf, where the highway crosses the water. Some genius has built a bird hide here out in the open, giving the birds every opportunity to escape when people approach.

Port Augusta can be good, too, for Red-backed Kingfishers and Rufous Fieldwrens. It is one of my favourite outback towns and when I'm there I always visit the Botanic Garden to reacquaint myself with the hooligan Chirruping Wedgebills.

Banded Stilt
Chirruping Wedgebill
Rufous Fieldwren
Singing Honeyeater

The Australian Arid Lands Botanic Garden in Port Augusta is the easiest place to see Chirruping Wedgebill.

Banded Stilts can often be seen huddled together in Spencer Gulf at Port Augusta.

48

Capertee Valley

Capertee Valley is 150 kilometres north-west of Sydney, or about three hours' drive. It is advertised as the world's second largest canyon, and the largest enclosed valley in the southern hemisphere, which seems a very odd claim to me. What matters is that it has great birding. It comprises eucalypt woodlands and Sydney's famous sandstone cliffs.

Birders visit the Capertee Valley in the hope of seeing a Regent Honeyeater. These are one of Australia's most stunning birds; no illustration ever seems able to capture their true beauty. Their presence depends on flowering eucalypts. Regent Honeyeaters are critically endangered and have suffered a serious population decline in recent decades. The population could be as low as 250 birds, notwithstanding a well-established captive breeding program. I didn't see any Regents when I visited.

I did see flocks of Turquoise Parrots. In Victoria, I'm excited to see one or two of these gorgeous birds; in the Capertee Valley, we saw flocks of more than a dozen birds. Other good birds here include Plum-headed Finches, Diamond Firetails and Sydney's sweet little specialty, the Rockwarbler.

Perhaps it's because I come from Melbourne, but I always get a thrill out of seeing Rockwarblers. Like me, these dear little cinnamon gems appreciate Sydney's sandstone. They are never far away from it.

There are both Grey and Pied Butcherbirds in the Capertee Valley, so visitors are bound to be treated to some marvellous music. Add carolling magpies

Turquoise Parrot
Rockwarbler
Black-chinned Honeyeater
AND, IF YOU'RE VERY LUCKY
Regent Honeyeater

Sulphur-crested Cockatoos screech across the Capertee Valley.

and mimicking lyrebirds and you'll have a veritable eisteddfod. Unless it's all drowned out by the screeches of Sulphur-crested Cockatoos or the cackles of kookaburras.

You could not visit Capertee without seeing Peaceful Doves, Crimson Rosellas and Jacky Winters. Of course, there are my favourites, Willie Wagtails and Grey Fantails. There are Crested Shriketits, Restless Flycatchers and White-winged Choughs.

There are plenty of honeyeaters, even if you dip on Regents. You are likely to see White-plumed and Black-chinned Honeyeaters, Noisy Friarbirds and Noisy Miners. There are also Yellow-tufted, Fuscous, Yellow-faced and White-naped. Vulnerable Brown Treecreepers are easily seen at Capertee. They are creeping up trees happily throughout the valley.

You can try to avoid House Sparrows, but you probably won't succeed. You'll see Red-browed and Double-barred Finches, and zebbies too. You might even see a Spotted Quail-thrush or a Powerful Owl.

Whether or not you're lucky enough to see Regent Honeyeaters, a trip to the Capertee Valley will provide a great deal of pleasure and some excellent birding. And you might see a flock of Turquoise Parrots.

Without a doubt one of our most glorious songsters, the Grey Butcherbird is easily seen (and heard) in the Capertee Valley.

With their characteristic sideways tail flick, Rockwarblers are often seen in the Capertee Valley.

49

Mission Beach

Mission Beach is famous as the spot to see Southern Cassowaries. Orange-footed Scrubfowl scratch the leaves with their oversized colourful feet as I admire their glamorous coiffed crest. Wompoo Fruit Doves make their extraordinary guttural call that Graham Pizzey records as paraphrased as 'bollocks are blue'. Gorgeous Olive-backed Sunbirds flitter around, adding a flourish of tropical extravagance, no less dazzling for being so common. On the beach, there's a chance of frigatebirds flying over, or Beach Stone-curlews loitering with intent. Or there might be a Pacific Reef Heron or an Osprey.

Mission Beach is a tourist town on Queensland's east coast, midway between Townsville and Cairns. It features picture postcard perfect beaches and dense tropical rainforest. The cassowaries are most often seen at Lacey Creek State Forest Park, ten kilometres from Mission Beach, or at nearby Licuala State Forest Park, decorated with huge fan-shaped licuala palms.

Last time we were there, we looked unsuccessfully for Red-necked Crakes. We saw several vibrant Ulysses butterflies, Fairy Gerygones, Forest Kingfishers and a Grey Goshawk. There were many Macleay's Honeyeaters playing among the leaves, surprisingly the only honeyeater we saw that day. We heard a most upsetting distress call from a frog and deduced it was being eaten by a snake. Australian Swiftlets swooped overhead and Pale Yellow Robins sat quietly watching us, minding their own business. We stood in a clearing for hours after dark being eaten by mosquitoes and hoping to see a Rufous Owl. All we saw were flying-foxes.

Self-effacing Grey Whistlers knew we were there, but chose not to interact with us. Rufous

Brown Cuckoo-Doves are found right down the east coast of mainland Australia, but they can be easily overlooked when they sit quietly.

Palm trees wave on idyllic Mission Beach.

Shrikethrushes, on the other hand, called in a friendly manner, and Superb Fruit Doves lived up to their name. There are Rose-crowned Fruit Doves here too. They are just as pretty and make a rapid 'hoo-hoo-hoo' call. Bar-shouldered Doves are quite common. Torresian Imperial Pigeons are easily seen – so big and so white – but Brown Cuckoo-Doves merge into the rainforest and are easily overlooked.

Like Australian King Parrots, male and female Australasian Figbirds must be about as sexually dimorphic as it's possible to be: the males at Mission Beach are bright yellow and green with a red facial mask, while females everywhere are brown with pretty streaked underparts. They seem to recognize each other and I guess that's all that matters.

I like Mission Beach, mozzies notwithstanding. I seem to see cassowaries about 50 per cent of the time. That's not bad for a species that's legally classified as vulnerable.

Southern Cassowaries are spectacular creatures by anyone's standards.

Southern Cassowary
Wompoo Fruit Dove
AND, IF YOU'RE LUCKY
Great Frigatebird
Pacific Baza

50

Bunyip State Park

Can there be a more famous helipad in Victoria than the one in Bunyip State Park? Birders go to this helipad at dusk in summer and wait for White-throated Nightjars to appear. It's that easy.

Melbourne birders know Bunyip State Park for two reasons: first, there's the famous helipad nightjar site; second, this is a beaut place to go spotlighting for Greater Sooty Owls.

In the past, Bunyip was home to wild populations of Victoria's critically endangered avifaunal emblem, the Helmeted Honeyeater. Alas, this is no longer the case. Helmeted Honeyeaters are a race of the common Yellow-tufted Honeyeater (they are slightly larger and even more gorgeous). In 2011, there were five breeding pairs in Bunyip State Park. Today, there are none.

White-throated Nightjar
Greater Sooty Owl
Eastern Yellow Robin
Pilotbird

Spotlighting is popular at Bunyip State Park, and Southern Boobooks are quite common.

This is Melbourne's most famous helipad, at Bunyip State Park, where birders come in summer to admire White-throated Nightjars.

While White-throated Nightjars are most accommodating, Greater Sooty Owls are another matter. For many years, Greater Sooty Owls were my jinx bird. Which is a bit of a joke, as I'd seen Lesser Sooty Owls at Julatten, and in those days Christidis and Boles infuriatingly refused to split them. So I spent many hours chasing a bird that wasn't even a tick. I heard them call in three different states, but I didn't manage to get a satisfying look until I gave in and hired a professional guide. He took me straight to Bunyip State Park.

Bunyip State Park, 65 kilometres east of Melbourne in the Dandenong Ranges, comprises 166 square kilometres of dense forest and swamps. The Bunyip River traverses the park. In 2018 devastating bushfires took their toll, remnants of which can still be seen today.

For night birds close to Melbourne, this is the place to go. Southern Boobooks are seen easily, as are the aforementioned nightjars. There are also Australian Owlet-nightjars, Powerful Owls and Tawny Frogmouths. There's even a chance of a Barking Owl.

The best bush birds in Bunyip include Beautiful Firetails, Pilotbirds and Large-billed Scrubwrens. The most common birds are Grey Fantails, White-throated Treecreepers, Brown Thornbills and Crimson Rosellas. There are also Red-browed Treecreepers and Blue-winged Parrots. Where there are Pilotbirds, there are Superb Lyrebirds, and Eastern Yellow Robins are everywhere. Scarlet and Rose Robins are common, too. Flame are rarer and Pink are difficult, but not impossible. There are both Pied and Grey Currawongs.

You'll see Superb Fairywrens and perhaps Southern Emu-wren. You'll certainly see Red Wattlebirds, White-eared and Yellow-faced Honeyeaters, and Eastern Spinebills. In fact, there are 16 species of honeyeater on the Bunyip bird list, including Lewin's and Crescent, and Scarlet Myzomela. You'll hear Yellow-tailed Black Cockatoos, even if you don't see them.

Bunyip is great for birding. There are also kangaroos, possums and gliders. And please always remain vigilant for bunyips.

Bunyip State Park is famous for Greater Sooty Owls – a bird it took me many years to see.

51

Serendip Sanctuary

You are bound to have fortuitous sightings in a place called Serendip. The name comes from 'serendipity', meaning 'the unexpected discovery of something wonderful'. Perhaps you'll see Beautiful Firetail, maybe a Pink Robin or a Pacific Koel, or even a Freckled Duck.

This 250-hectare property of open grassy woodlands and extensive wetlands is located 60 kilometres south-west of Melbourne and 22 kilometres north of Geelong. It is run by Parks Victoria and is open every day except Good Friday and Christmas Day. Entry is free. The sanctuary breeds Brolgas and Australian Bustards, and aviaries house several interesting species.

Serendip features resident populations of Magpie Geese and Cape Barren Geese. Pacific Black Duck, Grey and Chestnut Teal, Australian White Ibis and Yellow-billed Spoonbill are always present. Twitchers will be pleased to know that Eurasian Tree Sparrows are often seen here. As you stand surveying the wetlands, you'll hear the characteristic whistle of the Whistling Kite and Dusky Moorhens will scurry into the grass at the water's edge. A family of Superb Fairywrens cavorts in the grass and Masked Lapwings stand, statuesque, regarding you disdainfully.

Flocks of White-winged Choughs whistle and whir as they pass by. Red-rumped Parrots feed quietly in the grass, easily overlooked as you're distracted by a Little Eagle soaring above.

White-winged Chough
Black-fronted Dotterel
Common Bronzewing
Purple-crowned Lorikeet

Crested Pigeons have increased their range dramatically over recent years, and are now seen regularly at Serendip.

Magpie Geese have been bred at Serendip and there is now a resident population.

Black Kites are common at Serendip today. These birds are gradually extending their range. In my childhood they were considered rare in Victoria. I remember the first Black Kite I saw in this state. It was in the 1970s and I was driving up the Calder Highway towards Bendigo. At the time, it was exciting. Today, they are seen frequently in the western half of the state, and reliably at Serendip.

Other raptors seen often at Serendip are Brown Falcons and Collared Sparrowhawks. Wedge-tailed Eagles, Black Falcons, Brown Goshawks and Black-shouldered Kites are less regular, while Australian Hobbies, Peregrine Falcons, Spotted Harriers and Grey Goshawks are seen infrequently. Despite the extensive wetlands, there is not enough tall grass to encourage Swamp Harriers to take up residence.

Another bird that has extended its Victorian range dramatically in my lifetime is the Crested Pigeon. Previously restricted to the north of the state, it is now seen daily around Melbourne and regularly at Serendip.

Australasian Swamphens strut their stuff and Buff-banded Rail walk cautiously, never far from cover. Crakes have been seen here, but they're rare. Black-fronted Dotterels, on the other hand, are far from rare. They dash along the water's edge, pause for consideration, then dash off again. Fairy Martins spend summer here, arriving in October, building their beautiful mud nests, raising their young and leaving in February.

Altogether, there are lots of great birds. Let's face it, you have to be lucky in a place called Serendip.

Fairy Martins are summer visitors, arriving in spring, breeding, then leaving in late summer or early autumn.

Several western species venture as far east as Lake Gilles, such as this Rufous Treecreeper.

Lake Gilles Conservation Park

The first time Rog and I visited Lake Gilles Conservation Park was in October 1998. I was looking for Blue-breasted Fairywren which, until then, in my ignorance, I'd always thought were restricted to the south-west of Western Australia. I'm delighted to report that we found the bird easily. A family was hopping around happily as soon as we stopped the car. That's how I like birds to behave.

I was there again in October 2011 to admire the Blue-breasted Fairywren once more. This time I had wonderful views of Rufous Treecreepers and Gilbert's Whistlers, and found nests of Western Yellow Robin and Copperback Quail-thrush. The robin's nest was about 3 metres off

Lake Gilles Conservation Park is semi-arid mallee, with colourful wildflowers in spring.

Peter Waanders

the ground in a fork in a straggly mallee and was very beautifully decorated and well camouflaged. The quail-thrush's nest was on the ground and was surprisingly deep, much deeper than the textbook 'depression'. It contained two lovely splotchy eggs. I hurried away immediately to allow the bird to return to her nest duty.

On my most recent visit in 2022, my most interesting sighting was a young Striated Pardalote imitating a Copperback Quail-thrush.

Lake Gilles Conservation Park is 100 kilometres south-west of Port Augusta on the Eyre Highway, which actually passes through the park. It is always open and entry is free. The lake, which is quite large, is saline, so there are no waterbirds on the bird list. The park comprises 235 square kilometres of semi-arid mallee and is home to lots of remarkably colourful crested dragons. The spring flowers are colourful, too, and prolific. I remember mauve eremophila, red grevillea and hakea, yellow button bush and cream eucalyptus flowers.

We also saw some colourful birds: Splendid Fairywren, Rainbow Bee-eater, Australian Golden Whistler and Red-

Spiny-cheeked Honeyeaters have a wide distribution. They are pretty birds with a recognisable call.

capped Robin. Mulga Parrots flashed past and Australian Ringnecks were very common.

Apart from the ringnecks, the most common bird was the Spiny-cheeked Honeyeater. Their distinctive calls serenaded us all day. There were other honeyeaters too: Singing, Yellow-plumed and White-eared, as well as those big bullies, Red Wattlebirds. White-fronted, Brown-headed and Tawny-crowned are also on the list.

I love this semi-arid mallee, echoing with the calls of Crested Bellbirds. It's the sort of country you expect to see Emu running through. And we did. You also expect Grey Currawong, Grey Shrikethrush, Jacky Winter and Dusky Woodswallows.

We saw Chestnut-rumped, Yellow-rumped and Inland Thornbills, as well as Weebills and those pretty little jewels, Mistletoebirds.

Raptors are not very common in the park, although, astonishingly, Grey Falcon is on the list. We saw Wedge-tailed Eagles and Brown Goshawk. We also saw a splendid Red-backed Kingfisher.

Lake Gilles Conservation Park is the sort of place where you can see good birds at any time of year, and it's far enough west to accommodate western species like the Rufous Treecreeper, the Western Yellow Robin and the Blue-breasted Fairywren. A top spot indeed.

Crested Bellbird
Western Yellow Robin
Inland Thornbill
Local race of Australian Ringneck, known as Port Lincoln Parrot

Bruny Island

Bruny Island is famous among birders as the easiest place to see all Tasmania's endemics. With the possible exception of the Scrubtit, which often takes a bit of effort to find, they are all easily seen. Not only that, many desirable birds which can be found on the mainland, are more easily seen on Bruny. I'm thinking of Crescent Honeyeaters, Pink Robins and Beautiful Firetails. And also Hooded Plovers, Kelp Gulls and Black-faced Cormorants. Critically endangered Swift Parrots migrate to Tasmania to breed in summer and can still be seen here. The vulnerable Tasmanian race of Wedge-tailed Eagle is often seen on Bruny.

The narrow D'Entrecasteaux Channel separates Bruny Island from Tasmania. A ferry leaves from

Yellow-throated Honeyeaters are one of Tasmania's endemics, which are seen easily on Bruny Island.

Kettering, some 37 kilometres (or 40 minutes' drive) south of Hobart. The northern and southern parts of the island are joined by a very narrow neck. (This is the spot to go just after dark to see Little Penguins.) Altogether, the island is about 100 kilometres long and has a population of 600. The northern part of the island is mainly agricultural, but the south has much pristine bush, including South Bruny National Park.

Wherever you see manna gums, look for the endangered Forty-spotted Pardalote. These dear

A Brown Skua flies past the rugged cliffs of Bruny Island.

It's hard to miss the Tasmanian Nativehen, without doubt the easiest Tasmanian endemic to tick.

little birds forage unobtrusively in the canopy. They are not as noisy or as showy as Spotted Pardalotes, which are more numerous on Bruny. It is estimated that there are fewer than 700 Forty-spotted Pardalotes on Bruny and that the total population is around 1,800 and declining. Just to keep you on your toes, there are Striated Pardalotes here too. Some bright spark who knew more than nature, introduced Laughing Kookaburras to Tasmania. The kookaburras thrived and now include an occasional snack of Forty-spotted Pardalote in their varied menu.

Tasmanian Nativehens roam around both the north and south islands. Forest Ravens, Black Currawongs and Yellow-throated Honeyeaters are equally indiscriminate. Green Rosellas prefer forests or gardens and Dusky Robins like an ecotone – the zone where two habitats meet, perhaps the clearing at the edge of the bush. Yellow Wattlebirds like coastal heath and also gardens. Tasmania's other endemic honeyeaters (Black-headed and Strong-billed) prefer mature forests, so they'll be seen on the south island.

Bruny has a lot going for it – rugged coastline, pretty beaches, serene bush, very few people and wonderful birds.

Forty-spotted Pardalote
Yellow-throated Honeyeater
Tasmanian Nativehen
Black-headed Honeyeater

Azure Kingfishers are darling little jewels. I suspect they are present at Wonga Wetlands all year round. But I'm not sure, and will have to keep coming back to confirm this.

54 Wonga Wetlands

Wonga Wetlands, on the Murray River floodplain, provides habitat for many waterbirds.

Construction of the Hume Dam in 1919 stopped the natural flooding of the Murray River. Birds had nowhere to go. The Wonga Wetlands was created to rectify this error.

The wetlands are on the Corowa Road, 5.4 kilometres from Albury. The gates are open from 8.30 am until 4.30 pm on weekdays. Outside these times, you are welcome to go in on foot.

Wonga Wetlands cover 80 hectares of Murray River floodplain, and feature lagoons and billabongs and wonderful old river red gums. There are six bird hides (unfortunately, the noisy, unfriendly type) and three marked walks of varying lengths:

red 2.5 kilometres, blue 1.2 kilometres and green 0.5 kilometre.

Wonga Wetlands provide a bird list of 154 species which, it states, is 'probably incomplete'. I always find such an admission a challenge, but I haven't seen everything on the list and all I've managed to add are Peaceful Dove and Australian Pied Cormorant. This latter addition is apt as the name 'Wonga' means 'cormorant' in the Wiradjuri language, and indeed, all four of the Australian mainland cormorants are present.

Highlights of my visits to Wonga Wetlands include a Grest-crested Grebe in non-breeding plumage, Musk Ducks displaying, handsome Golden-headed Cisticola singing heartily, and, once,

back and collecting more data. What a burden.

Sacred Kingfishers are easier to determine: they are migratory. I've only seen them in spring and summer. They leave in autumn to spend the colder months up north.

Five species of crake and rail feature on the bird list (Buff-banded and Lewin's Rail, and Spotless, Australian and Baillon's Crake) but, look as I might, I've not seen any of them here. Nor have I ever seen a Glossy Ibis, although they are apparently common.

On one occasion, some people asked me to identify a Fan-tailed Cuckoo for them, and, in return, told me that they'd just seen a platypus from the footbridge. I hurried over as quietly as I could, but, like the crakes

Azure Kingfisher
Australian Reed Warbler (summer)
Royal Spoonbill
Olive-backed Oriole (summer)

This Australian Pied Cormorant is at his breeding best. 'Wonga' means 'cormorant' in the Wiradjuri language.

an irruption of Brown Quail. I often see Crested Shriketit and always tick Yellow Rosella. Twice I've seen White-breasted Woodswallows, one of my favourite birds.

I've only missed seeing gorgeous Azure Kingfishers on one occasion – that was in October 2009. As some populations of Azure Kingfishers are migratory and some are sedentary, I don't know if the Wonga Wetlands birds are really sedentary and I just didn't look hard enough that October, or whether they do migrate. I'll just have to keep going

and rails, the platypus eluded me.

There's an Aquatic Environment Education Centre at Wonga Wetlands provided by the Murray-Darling Freshwater Research Centre, Charles Sturt University and La Trobe University. I've often seen busloads of school groups enjoying a day out at the wetlands. I wonder if they appreciate how lucky they are. I went to school in the days of ink wells and free milk. How I would have loved to have been taken on an excursion to the Wonga Wetlands!

Black-faced Monarchs are found on the east coast of mainland Australia. They are summer migrants to Cabbage Tree Creek.

55

Cabbage Tree Creek Flora Reserve

In far east Gippsland's warm temperate rainforest stands an isolated population of Australia's most southerly, and Victoria's only, native palm, the Cabbage Tree Palm. The nearest palms to this odd isolated population are 180 kilometres away at Bega in New South Wales. Hence we have the Cabbage Tree Creek Flora Reserve. Access is either from the Princes Highway, 22 kilometres east of Orbost, or from the Marlo-Cabbage Tree Road. There is a short loop walk, which is often very wet underfoot.

The reserve provides a haven for many of our lovely temperate rainforest birds, such as Eastern Whipbirds, Superb Lyrebirds and White-throated

Victoria's only native palm occurs at Cabbage Tree Creek Flora Reserve.

Treecreepers. Eastern Yellow Robins and Rufous Fantails like this habitat, along with Crimson Rosellas, Satin Bowerbirds and Large-billed Scrubwrens. You'd expect Lewin's Honeyeaters, Australian Golden Whistlers and Wonga Pigeons. Yellow-tailed Black Cockatoos wail as they fly overhead. There are Scarlet Myzomelas, Rose Robins and Black-faced Monarchs. Fan-tailed Cuckoos trill and White-browed Scrubwrens scold angrily as they hop in the undergrowth. Small flocks of Silvereyes chase each other through the trees and Brown Gerygones hover like hummingbirds as they make their insect-like calls. Listen for the tinkle of Spotted Pardalotes and the beautiful liquid call of the Grey Shrikethrush. This unfortunate bird did nothing to deserve its unwelcome acronym: GST.

Crescent Honeyeaters are supposed to say 'Egypt', but I reckon the ornithologist who decided that probably moonlighted as a writer of creative fiction. The most common raptor is the Collared Sparrowhawk; they seem to like dense foliage to hide in more than most birds of prey. Grey Fantails are forever active, darting from branch to branch, ignoring the Laughing Kookaburra's chortle. If Grey Fantails are busy, Eastern Spinebills are hyperactive, never giving the birdwatcher a chance to focus her binoculars before they're off to their next appointment. Families of Superb Fairywrens hop cheerfully on the ground. It's difficult not to anthropomorphize when you see a superb blue male presenting a jenny with a carefully selected yellow flower. While you know what he's after, you can't help thinking what a charming gift.

Pied Currawongs fly overhead and Australian Magpies fill the air with wonderful carolling. Red Wattlebirds boss every bird in sight, thinking they're more important than everyone else. Brown Thornbills warble, and White-naped and Yellow-faced Honeyeaters feed together in the gum trees.

I have mentioned many species here and everything I've mentioned is common at Cabbage Tree Creek Flora Reserve. Next time you're travelling between Orbost and Cann River, the reserve is certainly worth a short deviation.

Spotted Pardalote (race *punctatus*)
Australian Golden Whistler
Brown Gerygone
Black-faced Monarch

There are both Red-browed and White-throated Treecreepers at Cabbage Tree Creek Flora Reserve, but White-throated (such as this) are far more common.

Strzelecki Track

Gibberbirds inhabit gibber plains and love the Strzelecki Track.

Birders want to tick all of the grasswrens. The Thick-billed is one of the easiest.

The Strzelecki Track no longer shares the romance of the Birdsville Track. Let's face it, since the advent of the Moomba gas fields, the Strzelecki is so well maintained, you can drive from one end to the other in a conventional car. Nevertheless, it is home to some very attractive birds and it is part of being Australian to experience the outback.

Many beautiful desert birds make their home along the Strzelecki Track. Birds such as Cinnamon Quail-thrush, Thick-billed Grasswren, and Orange and Crimson Chats. Perhaps the track is most famous for Chestnut-breasted Whiteface, although these dear little creatures are becoming harder to see as more and more zealous birders overwhelm them with tape recordings of their own song. As birders celebrate their success (or drown their failure) in the Lyndhurst Hotel, they are emboldened to hope for Letter-winged Kite by the sale of postcards depicting them – not a standard item for sale in an outback pub.

It's at Lyndhurst in the northern Flinders Ranges that the Strzelecki Track starts. It travels 466 kilometres through the Strzelecki Desert to Innamincka near the border of South Australia, Queensland and New South Wales. Innamincka is a friendly little town with a wonderful common full of coolabahs. I remember Diamond Doves, Tree Martins and Black-breasted Buzzards. Here, I was delighted to find a Crimson Chat's nest with two eggs in it. Little Corellas, Peaceful Doves, Black-faced Woodswallows, Black Kites and Australian Ringnecks were common. The ringnecks hereabouts say 'My mama done tole me'.

When Rog and I were there in August 2005, we detoured from Innamincka, 100 kilometres north-west to visit the Coongie Lakes. We saw Brolga, Masked Lapwing and Caspian Tern. We also saw Rufous Whistlers, a Great Egret and, most special, a Rufous-crowned Emu-wren, right on the southern limit

of its range. On the way back to Innamincka, we saw Cinnamon Quail-thrush, always a joy, even though we saw so many.

We camped beside Cooper Creek and watched Whistling Kites breaking dead twigs off live trees to use for nesting material. While we watched, a Brolga landed in the water in front of us. City life seemed a long way away.

Along the track, as well as Cinnamon Quail-thrush, we saw Little Buttonquail, Emus, Hooded Robins and Singing Honeyeaters. Brown Songlarks and Chirruping Wedgebills were constant companions, along with Willie Wagtails and Eastern Bluebonnets. We saw Australian Pratincole standing erect and proud, while Nankeen Kestrels hovered overhead and majestic Wedge-tailed Eagles recycled any unlucky roadkill. Australian Bustards strutted their stuff with their supercilious manner and wherever there was a skerrick of water, we'd see White-necked Herons, Black-fronted Dotterels and Maned Duck. Magpie-larks and Crested Pigeons were everywhere.

The outback without roughing it – Cinnamon Quail-thrush and Chestnut-breasted Whiteface. Sounds like heaven to me.

Cinnamon Quail-thrush
Orange Chat
AND, IF YOU'RE LUCKY
Thick-billed Grasswren
Chestnut-breasted
 Whiteface

Wedge-tailed Eagles are often seen in the outback gathered at roadkill.

It's great to stand on top of the hill and watch Australian Shelducks fly past at eye level.

57 Tower Hill Wildlife Reserve

Tower Hill Wildlife Reserve is a revegetated long-extinct volcano.

Sue Taylor

To me, Tower Hill means Emus, koalas and kangaroos. And an opportunity to see many bush birds and waterbirds.

Warrnambool is 264 kilometres west of Melbourne and Tower Hill Wildlife Reserve is 14 kilometres west of Warrnambool on the Princes Highway. The reserve is open 24 hours and admission is free. This revegetated, long extinct volcano is a real conservation success story. When planting began in the 1960s, the site had been denuded by overgrazing. Today you can see the results as you drive through on the safe one-way road. Keep an eye on the rocky cliff face for a white splash, indicative of a roosting raptor, perhaps a Peregrine Falcon.

There's a tower on top of the hill (which presumably explains the name) and it's always worth checking this out for raptors too. You could see a Whistling or Black-shouldered Kite, or a Nankeen Kestrel. Swamp Harriers sometimes fly low over the water and wedgies sometimes soar very high overhead.

I don't think I've ever been to Tower Hill without seeing Emus. I always see Black Swans too, and Pacific Black Ducks and White-browed Scrubwrens. There are usually Australian Shelducks; it's great to stand on top of the hill and watch them fly past at eye level.

You'll see Chestnut and Grey Teal and Hardhead, and maybe Musk Duck will put on a splashing display for you. White-faced Heron usually hunt in the shallows and Australian White Ibis decorate dead trees. There can be big flocks of Eurasian Coots on the water, and Australasian Swamphen strut around the shoreline. Both Masked Lapwings and Magpie-larks play along the edge, while Pied Stilts admire their reflections in the water. The reserve is not far from the sea and Silver Gulls are often present. You'll probably hear the mournful three-note whistle of the Little Grassbird coming from the reeds, while you watch Welcome Swallows hawking over the water.

Long-billed Corellas are common – listen for their discordant quavering call. You may see Crimson Rosellas and will certainly observe Superb Fairywrens. The most common honeyeaters are New Holland, followed by Yellow-faced and White-naped. Silvereyes are one of my favourite bush birds, and they are common,

as are Grey Fantails. There are lots of European Goldfinches and Red-browed Finches. In summer you can see Rufous Whistlers and Satin Flycatchers and you can enjoy the rich melodious song of the Grey Shrikethrush at any time.

So next time you go whale watching at Warrnambool, allow time to visit Tower Hill and see if it's possible to visit without seeing an Emu.

Emu
Australian Shelduck
White-browed Scrubwren
Superb Fairywren

In eastern Australia, White-naped Honeyeaters wear orange eye make-up.

Tarra-Bulga National Park in Gippsland, in eastern Victoria, is the place to go to see Pilotbirds. They hang around obligingly in the Bulga car park (note that this is not the Visitor Information Centre car park). Tarra-Bulga is also one of the easiest places to see Superb Lyrebirds. It used to be thought that you didn't see Pilotbirds without accompanying lyrebirds. Indeed, the Pilotbirds were thought to be guiding the lyrebirds or piloting them around. Hence the name. Ornithologists are no longer quite so gullible, and Pilotbirds in the presence of lyrebirds are now thought to be hanging around for a free lunch – taking advantage of the larger bird's scratching for grubs.

Tarra-Bulga National Park is in the Strzelecki Ranges, 200 kilometres east of Melbourne, and comprises over 2,000 hectares of cool temperate rainforest and mountain ash forest. To get there, turn off the Princes Highway at Traralgon and follow the signs. Roads are winding and narrow, and are used by inappropriately large logging trucks. Views are usually impressive, although

Without a doubt, the Bulga car park is the easiest place to see Pilotbirds.

Tarra-Bulga is a great place to see Superb Lyrebirds and winter is the best season when they are most vocal.

after the Black Saturday fires in 2009, the devastation was horrific. Luckily, the national park escaped the fires. There are several walks in Tarra-Bulga National Park, the longest being Forest Track, which is 4.4 kilometres and takes one and a half hours. It has some steep sections. There's another track through rainforest which just takes 35 minutes and takes you past crystal-clear brooks and a pretty waterfall. The Nature Walk takes 15 minutes, and has interpretative signs. I used to set off from the Bulga car park and walk to the Visitor Information

Centre, where Roger used to pick me up. If I didn't deviate to the suspension bridge or get distracted by lyrebirds or whipbirds, this would take about 20 minutes. It is an easy walk and there are seats provided, where you can sit and listen to a lyrebird or watch Silvereyes foraging among the ferns. Superb Fairywrens hop around on the forest floor and Brown Thornbills chatter above.

The magnificent mountain ash is the world's tallest flowering plant, growing up to an impressive 95 metres. The cool fern gullies also feature ancient myrtle beech, banyallas, southern sassafras, austral mulberry and an impressive 41 different species of fern.

The Tarra-Bulga bird list comprises 106 species, of which 54 are present all year round. This is the closest place to

Melbourne I know to see Brown Gerygones reliably and there are Large-billed as well as White-browed Scrubwren. I always see yellow robins and black cockies, usually Bassian Thrush and Australian Golden Whistlers and, if I'm lucky, a Pink or a Rose Robin. I have to look carefully at the treecreepers, as both Red-browed and White-throated are found here. In the picnic area there are often Laughing Kookaburras and Crimson Rosellas.

Tarra-Bulga is a very pleasant spot, which I would never have found if I hadn't been looking for Pilotbirds. And it goes without saying that the lyrebirds are superb.

Tarra-Bulga National Park comprises mountain ash forest and cool temperate rainforest.

Superb Lyrebird
Pilotbird
Yellow-tailed Black
   Cockatoo
Crescent Honeyeater

Barrington Tops National Park

One of Australia's three mound builders, Australian Brushturkeys are common at Barrington Tops.

Rose Robin
Brown Cuckoo-Dove
Yellow-throated Scrubwren
AND, IF YOU'RE VERY LUCKY
Rufous Scrubbird

Barrington Tops National Park is a World Heritage Area that boasts both snow and rainforest.

It's odd to think of rainforest and snow occurring in the same national park, and yet this happens at Barrington Tops. It is one of the largest temperate rainforests on mainland Australia, located in New South Wales north of Newcastle near Gloucester. It's a World Heritage Area. The highest point is over 1,500 metres and yes, it can snow in winter.

Birders go to Barrington Tops National Park in the hope of ticking the elusive Rufous Scrubbird. I can confirm that there are scrubbirds present – I've heard them. I spent three days looking for them one September. It was very cold (5 °C) and it rained every day. I heard several scrubbirds, but didn't stand a chance of seeing them in the dense scrub. I tried standing still near the creek where the birds were calling. I tried chasing them through the scrub. I could feel them looking at me scornfully before they ran away laughing. 'We won', they chuckled again and again. I returned again in Octobeer 2014 with professional help and finally had great views of scrubbirds.

On our first visit Rog and I stayed in a motel in Gloucester where there were Grey-crowned Babblers in the garden. Both Pacific Black and Maned Ducks were nesting in the gum trees and hundreds of Eastern Cattle Egrets foraged in adjacent paddocks.

To get to the national park, you must make six river crossings. The water isn't very deep, so they haven't bothered to build bridges. You just splash through. Red-necked wallabies watched our progress with indifference – they'd seen it all before.

We stopped for coffee in the picnic grounds, rain and cold temperatures notwithstanding. We watched Superb Lyrebirds and Rose Robins as we clutched our mugs in an effort to warm up. We saw Wonga Pigeons, Lewin's Honeyeaters and Brown Cuckoo-Doves, but there was not a hint of Satin Flycatchers, even though it was spring, the best time to look for them. Nor did we see any Olive Whistlers. Frankly, we were lucky to see anything in that bleak, unfriendly weather.

Willie Wagtails weren't daunted by the conditions. Nor were Bar-shouldered Doves, or Australian Brushturkeys. We saw Australian King Parrots and both Eastern and Crimson Rosellas, and Flame and Eastern Yellow Robins. We saw Australian Golden Whistlers, Restless Flycatchers and Spotted Pardalotes. Red-browed Finches played on the ground, along with Superb Fairywrens and White-browed Scrubwrens. Yellow, Brown and Yellow-rumped Thornbills all flitted from tree to tree and the mournful eerie call of White-winged Choughs echoed through the forest. I was surprised to note that Russet-tailed Thrush was on the bird list, along with Bassian Thrush. Barrington Tops was not very welcoming. The weather was foul and the scrubbirds were infuriating. But anywhere you can sit and watch Superb Lyrebirds and Rose Robins while having morning coffee is okay by me.

The Russet-tailed Thrush
can be shy and elusive.

Providence Petrels fly over Mount Lidgbird on Lord Howe Island.

60 Lord Howe Island

I loved Lord Howe Island. I've been there just once, in March 1996. The temperatures were perfect, the scenery was stunning, the people were friendly and the birding was excellent. I was excited to see the woodhen, back from the brink of extinction, and fascinated at the way Providence Petrels responded to shouting. I remember colourful day lilies, lots of golden orb spiders and Sacred Kingfishers, and a couple of Pacific Golden Plovers on the airfield dressed up in their breeding best.

But the bird that stole my heart, quite unexpectedly, was the White Tern. They fluttered above our heads like fairies, with ethereal pure white plumage, their big black eyes making them look both beautiful and intelligent. They don't build a nest, laying their single egg directly onto the branch of a tree. Naturally there are many fatalities.

Lord Howe Island is part of New South Wales and is located 700 kilometres north-east of Sydney, 500 kilometres due east of Port Macquarie. It took us two hours to fly there in a Dash 8. The island is tiny – a total of 1,344 hectares, just 11 kilometres from one end to the other, and a few hundred metres across at the most narrow point. Accommodation is either self-contained apartments or lodges.

The saga of rats on Lord Howe Island was a sad tale. I'm delighted to say that now they have been eradicated, quite an impressive effort. They were introduced accidentally in 1918. Within a few years, five birds were extinct: a warbler, the fantail, Robust White-eye, Vinous-tinted Blackbird and Lord Howe Starling. Buff-banded Rails were exterminated by rats but reintroduced themselves in the 1970s and are now quite numerous. Masked Owls, which we used to be told were introduced to control the rats, prefer to snack on easier prey – such as White Terns, Black-winged Petrels, Providence Petrels and woodhens.

The success of the captive breeding program for woodhen is well known. The population was down to ten breeding pairs when captive breeding began in 1979. Feral pigs were eradicated before birds were released back into the wild. Since rat eradication, the population of woodhen is estimated to be 230.

We visited Muttonbird Point, where there is a seabird viewing platform. It was a hard walk, but the Sooty Terns and Masked Boobies with babies made it worth it. We went to Malabar for Red-tailed Tropicbirds, Little Island for Providence Petrels and Lord Howe Woodhen, and admired shearwaters from Signal Point (Wedge-tailed on Rabbit Island) and Middle Beach (Flesh-footed and Little on the

I fell in love with the ethereal White Terns.

Admiralty Islets). We also saw Black-winged Petrels from Middle Beach. We did a boat trip to North Beach, where I photographed Brown Noddies – they lived up to their name and were so stupid I could walk right up to them.

All Australian birders simply must visit Lord Howe Island. But not between June and September, because there aren't any White Terns here then.

Lord Howe Woodhen
White Tern (October to May)
Red-tailed Tropicbird
Brown Noddy

One of Australia's best conservation success stories, the Lord Howe Woodhen is now easily seen.

61

Buffalo Creek

Buffalo Creek is probably the most unlikely birding site in this book. The spot I have in mind is actually a very popular boat-launching ramp with its associated car park, and on weekends there is a constant coming and going of cars, boats and fishermen. It is 18 kilometres north of Darwin, accessed via Lee Creek Road. It may not look much, but anywhere I've got a lifer is all right with me.

Above the cacophony of boat launching, we heard the unmistakable raucous call of a Chestnut Rail. We looked in the direction of the call and the rail strutted into sight! Then a boat blocked my view. I rushed to reposition myself. The rail stood quite still on the muddy bank, totally oblivious to the mayhem around him. I had excellent views, before he decided he'd had enough and slowly turned and strutted back into the mangroves. I glimpsed other rails that morning, but none were quite as generous with their time as that first beautiful bird.

At the car park, we saw Greater Crested and Caspian Terns, and Silver Gulls. A Pacific Emerald Dove wandered among the cars as unimpressed with human activity as the Chestnut Rail had

Lemon-bellied Flyrobins build the smallest nest of any bird.

Our largest rail, the Chestnut, seems to have adapted to boats and fisherfolk at Buffalo Creek.

Chestnut Rail
Green-backed Gerygone
Lemon-bellied Flyrobin
Red-winged Parrot

been. So did a Magpie-lark, but I guess I'm used to that. Red-winged Parrots, Torresian Imperial Pigeons and Torresian Crows flew overhead, and on the mud we saw Eurasian Whimbrels and Common Sandpipers. In the bushes we saw Green-backed Gerygones, Grey Whistlers and Canary White-eyes.

A Lemon-bellied Flyrobin sat on her tiny nest and overflowed. This is the smallest nest of any bird. No wonder she lays only one egg.

We saw Spangled Drongos and White-bellied Cuckooshrikes. White-breasted Woodswallows clustered on a branch and a Little Bronze Cuckoo flew by, wanting to get onto my bird list. We saw Brown and White-gaped Honeyeaters, Tree Martins and Bar-shouldered Doves. A Forest Kingfisher sat in the mangroves, aware of how handsome he looked. Rainbow Lorikeets flew over, squawking, just to make sure they were noticed.

Now that's not bad for a car park, is it? The bird list for Buffalo Creek comprises 154 species.

There are some common birds usually seen here that we missed out on, such as Black and Whistling Kites, Orange-footed Scrubfowl, Rainbow Bee-eaters and Red-headed Myzomelas. Nice birds, all of them.

But hey, with such a great view of a Chestnut Rail, who's complaining?

Buffalo Creek, near Darwin, is the best spot to see Chestnut Rails.

133

62

Ku-ring-gai Chase National Park

for the bush birds: pigeons and parrots, cuckoos and cockatoos (the best being Glossy Blacks), cheerful little Silvereyes, friendly Grey Fantails and confiding Eastern Yellow Robins. Sydney's specialty, the Rockwarbler, can be found here, as can the much sought-after Chestnut-rumped Heathwren. There are Eastern Whipbirds, Australian Golden Whistlers and even Superb Lyrebirds. And, best of all, a cornucopia of honeyeaters.

There are 18 species of honeyeater on the Ku-ring-gai Chase bird list, which is not a bad total considering the park is so close to Australia's largest city. Of course, I'm partisan – both my favourite honeyeaters are here – White-eared

Common at Ku-ring-gai Chase, the Grey Shrikethrush is one of our most glorious songsters.

Just 25 kilometres north of Sydney, Ku-ring-gai Chase National Park is home to 126 species of bird.

The bush is filled with fluty melodious calls of the Grey Shrikethrush. Dressed most modestly, this bird makes up for his unassuming attire by his delightfully tuneful song. We should not take these glorious songsters for granted just because they are common.

We are standing in Ku-ring-gai Chase National Park, 25 kilometres north of Sydney. I have two special memories of this place: the unexpected sighting of an Australian Brushturkey, and a magnificent specimen of a flowering waratah. Silver Gulls squabble on the beaches of Pittwater, and ducks and cormorants quietly enjoy the waters of the Hawkesbury River. We're here and Brown-headed. The White-eared is the most common. It really is a most striking bird – black and white and bright olive-green. To make up for its handsome appearance, it has a loud, not particularly attractive call. Brown-headeds are not striking at all. They are very quietly pretty, companionable and captivating, quite different from most of the aggressive sugar-laden bullies of the honeyeater world, such as Red Wattlebirds and Noisy Miners.

Everyone loves Eastern Spinebills. With their long down-turned bill, they were made to feature on postcards and calendars. The one shown here is a juvenile and hasn't yet developed the adult's stunning throat pattern.

Yellow-tufted and Scarlet Myzomelas add a flamboyant touch of colour, and White-naped and Yellow-faced Honeyeaters migrate together. It's always a challenge to see the orange eye-ring on the White-naped as he hangs upside down among the foliage. There are both New Holland and White-cheeked Honeyeaters here, two very good-looking birds. You'll probably hear the Noisy Friarbirds living up to their name before you see them.

Blue-faced Honeyeaters are easily identified, but not very common here. Tawny-crowned, White-plumed and Fuscous are not particularly numerous either. Lewin's Honeyeaters are plentiful enough and Little Wattlebirds are common.

So there you have 18 species. You could spend a day at Ku-ring-gai Chase simply studying honeyeaters.

This young Eastern Spinebill has not yet developed adult plumage.

Rockwarbler
White-cheeked Honeyeater
Australian Golden Whistler
AND, IF YOU'RE LUCKY
Chestnut-rumped Heathwren

Hattah-Kulkyne National Park

63

Chestnut Quail-thrushes are usually easily seen along the Nowingi Track.

Emus enjoy their evening drink at Lake Konardin in Hattah-Kulkyne National Park.

Birders know the Nowingi Track in Hattah-Kulkyne National Park only too well. Most of us have spent many hours traversing it, looking for Striated Grasswren and Mallee Emu-wren. The first Chestnut Quail-thrush we see is greeted with joy. The second is also welcomed warmly. By about the sixth, birders are silently wishing a few Quail-thrush might be converted to grasswren.

The township of Hattah is on the Calder Highway, about 480 kilometres north-west of Melbourne and about 70 kilometres south of Mildura. Entry to the national park is well signposted and about four kilometres east of Hattah. The park is 48,000 hectares, stretching between the highway and the Murray River. There are some

Chestnut Quail-thrush
Mallee Emu-wren
Regent Parrot
AND, IF YOU ARE LUCKY
Striated Grasswren

*Like most grasswrens, the
Striated can prove difficult
to observe.*

lovely nature drives among the cypress pine and black box, where you can spot Emus and admire flocks of Major Mitchell's Cockatoos. Without much imagination, these comedic birds used to be called 'Pink Cockatoos'. The race found here is arguably prettier than their western relatives, wearing a yellow stripe in their crest.

There are several lakes at Hattah, fed by Chalka Creek, an anabranch of the Murray. Hence there are many waterbirds on the bird list: ducks, grebes, cormorants, herons, egrets, spoonbills and even the White-bellied Sea Eagle. There can also be Australian Crakes and Black-tailed Nativehens. I've seen enormous flocks of nativehens here running around in the grass like chooks.

Red-lored Whistlers are on the list, as are Grey-crowned Babblers. However, you are much more likely to see Gilbert's Whistlers and White-browed Babblers. Scarlet-chested Parrots are on the list too, but they are rarely seen. Black-eared Miners also appear on the list, but it is uncertain whether there are still any here that have not contaminated their genes by interbreeding with Yellow-throated Miners.

What you will see are Galahs, Sulphur-crested Cockatoos, Grey Currawongs and the yellow-rumped race of Spotted Pardalotes. There are Striated Pardalotes too. You will see Spiny-cheeked, White-eared and Yellow-plumed Honeyeaters, and both Noisy and Yellow-throated Miners. Blue-faced Honeyeaters and Grey Butcherbirds may join you for lunch if you sit at a popular picnic table.

One beautiful bird that there is a very good chance of seeing is the eastern race of the Regent Parrot, officially classified as vulnerable. These gorgeous golden birds sit quietly in the river red gums, or walk up the limbs like tightrope walkers.

Hattah is a very peaceful place. What could be nicer than a cold beer on a hot night, sitting beside Lake Konardin watching Emus come in for their evening drink?

Spotless Crakes are quite common at Fivebough Swamp at Leeton.

64 Fivebough Swamp, Leeton

Leeton, in the New South Wales Riverina, is 550 kilometres west of Sydney. It is an interesting little town with striking art deco architecture. Of more interest to birders is the 400-hectare swamp on the outskirts of town.

Here there is a good chance of seeing a crake – either Baillon's, Australian or Spotless. There's also a very good chance of seeing Brolga, Red-necked Avocets, Purple-backed Fairywren and Golden-headed Cisticolas. How's that for a list of desirable, beautiful birds! There's a slight chance you might spot a Zebra Finch.

I saw Red-capped Robins (always a favourite), a Little Grassbird, an Australian Reed Warbler, a hare, a water rat and far too many golden orb spiders. I confided in my diary that the management of these wetlands spend more money on brochures than they do on maintenance. Wattles had grown up in front of the bird hides, and I couldn't see a thing. I had no chance of seeing a crake or a Brolga.

Birding friends tell me that this problem has since been rectified and I include the site here on that basis. After all, there are 180 birds on the bird list. They are good birds too. I saw White-breasted Woodswallows, Silvereyes, Little Friarbirds and a Pallid Cuckoo.

Of course there are all the common waterbirds. The most abundant bird is the Black Swan, followed by the Pied Stilt. All the usual ducks and ibis are present, along with pelicans, plovers and dotterels, swamphens, moorhens and coots. As you'd expect, there are White-faced Herons, Great Egrets, Royal Spoonbills and Black-tailed Nativehens. And, as soon as you have a good swamp, you're bound to have Swamp Harriers. Other common raptors include Whistling Kites and Nankeen Kestrels. I saw a Peregrine Falcon flying overhead at great speed, but I'm not sure how often they're seen here.

As well as the common ducks you'd expect to see, there are other, special, waterfowl. Ducks such as Australasian Shovelers, Pink-eared, Blue-billed, Musk and even Freckled Ducks. And the ibis are not just your usual Australian White and Straw-necked; they also include Glossy Ibis. You might even luck onto an Australasian Bittern or a Black-backed Bittern or an Australian Painted-snipe. Even the rare and elusive Grey Falcon has been reported here!

Next time I visit, I expect to come away with a bird list crammed full of crakes and bitterns and I'll forget my unpleasant experience of spiders and overgrown wattles.

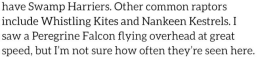

Baillon's Crake
Brolga
Little Grassbird
White-breasted Woodswallow

When the male Musk Duck displays, he makes an unusual high-pitched whistle that doesn't sound like a duck at all.

Baillon's Crakes are tiny, but much sought after and frequently seen at Fivebough.

65

Little Desert National Park

The local race of Australian Ringnecks, called 'Mallee Ringnecks', is common, but delightful nonetheless.

The Little Desert National Park was proclaimed primarily to protect the Malleefowl.

When I was young, my parents took me to meet Keith Hateley at the Little Desert National Park. Keith was devoted to the survival and wellbeing of the Malleefowl and was delighted to show us his favourite pair of Malleefowl, Romeo and Juliet. We lay on the ground, perfectly still, only partly hidden by the scrubby mallee, with sticks poking into us and ants invading our private parts. We waited and waited and waited and were eventually rewarded with the imperial presence of Romeo. He tended his mound, adjusting the temperature by adding or removing sand and rotting leaves, until it was just right for Juliet to lay her eggs.

Malleefowl are fascinating birds. They are regal creatures with a stately step and exquisitely dappled plumage that camouflages them perfectly in the mottled mallee. Due mainly to destruction of habitat, they are classified as vulnerable. Sadly, Keith Hateley is no longer with us today, but all his good work is commemorated with a Nature Walk in his name.

It was primarily to protect the Malleefowl that 136,000 hectares were set aside as the Little Desert National Park in 1968, following some controversial suggestions that the land be opened up for farming. Again, it was chiefly because of the Malleefowl that BirdLife International nominated the Little Desert as an Important Bird Area. In doing so, BirdLife International noted that the park was home to from ten to 20 breeding pairs of Malleefowl, as well as important populations of Southern Scrub Robins and Diamond Firetails.

The park is located 375 kilometres west of Melbourne and comprises mallee heathland, with some cypress pine and casuarina woodlands. A desert is not defined by the presence of heat and sand; it is defined by its annual rainfall, which must be less than 254 millimetres. So, with rainfall of 400 millimetres each year, the so-called Little Desert isn't a desert at all. But it looks like one. And it certainly has heat and sand.

Good birds here include Black-eared Cuckoo, Gilbert's Whistler, and Red-capped and Hooded Robins. The local race of Australian Ringnecks are known as Mallee Ringnecks. They are common, but delightful nevertheless. Slender-billed Thornbills are seen here, along with several desirable honeyeaters: Purple-gaped, White-fronted, Tawny-crowned and Striped. Emus stroll among the wildflowers, seemingly oblivious to their beauty.

It's not just because of happy childhood memories that I love the Little Desert. I love this dry understated country with its occasional unexpected flash of colour. And I love the Malleefowls.

Malleefowl are most stately as they strut their stuff.

Malleefowl
Southern Scrub Robin
Diamond Firetail
Shy Heathwren

66

Sturt National Park

Bourke's Parrots wear beautifully subtle delicate colouring.

saw a surprising number of waterbirds.

We saw several species of honeyeater, including White-fronted, Black and Pied, and four species of Woodswallow: Masked, White-browed, White-breasted and Black-faced. Although we dipped on the Grey Falcon, we did see eight species of raptor.

We noted several familiar birds with unfamiliar calls, namely Spiny-cheeked Honeyeater, Crested Bellbird and Red-capped Robin. I thought that the mournful whistle of the Pied Honeyeater was reminiscent of the call of the Little Grassbird.

There are a couple of interesting drives. The first is the Jump Up Loop Road, which is 47 kilometres and starts off the Silver City Highway at South Myers Tank. We saw Banded Lapwings, Eastern Bluebonnets and Purple-backed Fairywren on this drive. The other is the Gorge Loop Road, which commences at the Mount Wood Homestead. We saw Wedge-tailed Eagle, Black-fronted Dotterel, Crested Bellbird, Pied Butcherbird and Australian Pipit here.

Some birds are easy ticks – go to the right locale at the right time and you are rewarded effortlessly. Other birds take some work. In our case, the Flock

The first time we visited Sturt National Park, we ticked Bourke's Parrot, Crimson Chat and Flock Bronzewing. The second time we visited, we ticked Chestnut-breasted Quail-thrush. Of course, we were looking for Grey Grasswren and Grey Falcon, but we had no luck with either bird on either occasion.

Sturt National Park comprises 340,000 hectares of desert and semi-desert, well stocked with Emus and red kangaroos. You must pay to enter the park. It is in the far north-west of New South Wales, 330 kilometres north of Broken Hill. The park is littered with isolated mesas, which the locals call 'jump ups', and which rise up to 150 metres above the flat gibber plains. There are red sand dunes and dry creek beds bordered with red gums, acacias and coolabahs. Don't even think of going in summer – it's way too hot. Given the terrain, we

After a good season, Flock Bronzewing can irrupt at Sturt National Park.

Flock Bronzewing
Bourke's Parrot
Crimson Chat
AND, IF YOU ARE VERY LUCKY
Grey Grasswren

Gaudy Crimson Chats are quite common in Sturt National Park.

Bronzewing required a bit of effort. When we did the Jump Up Loop Road drive, we noticed a bird hide at South Myers Tank and we thought it a likely spot. We turned up at about five in the evening with a can of cold beer each. Although this was only September, it was hot. At 6.30, I'd run out of beer and patience. I stood to go and that was the cue for a pair of Flock Bronzewings to fly in for their evening drink. Suddenly, I didn't notice the heat and instead of cold beer I drank in the beautiful bronzewings.

While I was looking for Grey Grasswrens, I saw White-winged Fairywrens, Chirruping Wedgebills, Singing Honeyeaters and Orange Chats. I'd have happily swapped them all for a grasswren.

I have lovely memories of Sturt National Park: the purple eremophilla at our campsite; Bourke's Parrots nesting in a dead gum tree; but, most of all, those delightfully dappled Flock Bronzewing.

67

Norfolk Island

When I think of Norfolk Island, I think of Norfolk Island pines and the mutiny on the *Bounty*. The pines are beautiful – tall and regal. Lichen decorates them like Christmas tinsel. But I didn't go there for the botany; I went there for the birds.

Norfolk Island boasts five birds that cannot be seen anywhere else in Australia. And then there are seabirds. And there is always the possibility of a rarity.

Norfolk Island is just eight kilometres long and five kilometres wide, making a total land area of 3,855 hectares (which makes it about three times the size of Lord Howe Island). It's located about 1,000 kilometres from the eastern coast of Australia. It takes two hours 45 minutes to fly there from Sydney. To the south of Norfolk, there are two small uninhabited islands, Philip and Nepean, which are both very important seabird rookeries. Norfolk Island has a subtropical temperate climate. When we were there for a week in July 2004, it wasn't cold, but it rained every day.

The five special birds are: the California Quail (introduced admittedly, but not usually found quite so easily anywhere else in Australia); the Norfolk Parakeet (formerly called the Tasman and before that the Red-crowned Parakeet and locally known as the Green Parrot to distinguish it from introduced Crimson Rosellas, called Red Parrots); the Norfolk Gerygone (sometimes called the Grey Gerygone, common and widespread); the Norfolk Robin (formerly called the Pacific Robin and originally the type specimen for the mainland Scarlet Robin); and the Slender-billed White-eye (larger than the mainland Silvereye, but more slender with bright yellow underparts). The Norfolk Parakeet proved elusive. Which is hardly surprising, as there are only 438 of them (such precision!). However, the population is well managed and is increasing, so the conservation status is no higher than vulnerable. I heard them before I saw them: 'kek-kek-kek'. To me, it sounded like the beginning of a Laughing Kookaburra's call. I finally saw them on a very wet walk from Mount Pitt to Palm Glen. Another bird that lured birders to Norfolk Island in the past was the White-chested White-eye. Sad to say, they are now officially extinct.

There are two other local passerines that birders will want to see: the Grey Fantail and the Australian Golden Whistler. Male Australian Golden Whistlers

Norfolk Island's rugged coastline is very picturesque.

The endangered Norfolk Robin is only found on Norfolk Island.

on Norfolk Island are not golden at all – they wear female plumage with yellow undertail coverts.

No respectable birder is going to travel over 1,000 kilometres to see a feral goose (common around Kingston) or the rare Norfolk Island Morepork Owl (which is a hybrid between the Norfolk Boobook and New Zealand's Morepork). But birders can hope for a Long-tailed Cuckoo. They breed in New Zealand in summer, then migrate north for the winter. Some pass through Norfolk Island in March, but sightings are not common.

As to seabirds, Norfolk Island is the easiest place for Australian birders to add Grey Noddies (that we used to call Grey Ternlets), and Black-winged and White-necked Petrels to their lifelists, and everyone wants to see the Masked Boobies as many people believe they will soon be recognized as a separate species, the Tasman Booby.

Norfolk Island is steeped in history. It is clinically clean and picturesque. And you can expect at least five lifers.

The Norfolk Parakeet, locally known as the 'Green Parrot', might be in serious trouble.

Norfolk Gerygone
Norfolk Robin
Slender-billed White-eye
AND, IF YOU'RE LUCKY
Norfolk Parakeet

Terns can be difficult to identify. Here, the crimson bill and grey belly help to identify a Whiskered Tern.

68

Lake Cargelligo sewage treatment works

Lake Cargelligo is in central New South Wales, about 600 kilometres west of Sydney. I happened across it by accident on my way to Round Hill Nature Reserve. There was a large flock of Red-necked Avocets on the lake and Mulga Parrots flew by, so I stopped to have a look. The sewage works are south of the township near the showgrounds and can provide some exciting birding with possible sightings of Blue-billed Ducks and Peregrine Falcons.

Flocks of Cockatiels wheel overhead as you admire Pied Stilts and Red-kneed Dotterels.

Australasian Swamphen strut around the shoreline and Willie Wagtails chatter noisily, always hyperactive, wanting to draw attention to themselves. Eurasian Coots are plentiful, as are Dusky Moorhens and Black-tailed Nativehens. Crested Pigeons coo softly behind you as you watch Baillon's Crake walking quietly right out into the open. Soon they are joined by Australian and Spotless Crakes. All three crakes are common here.

A Whistling Kite makes his characteristic whistle – an odd sound for such a big bird. Wood Sandpipers stand quietly at the water's edge and Pink-eared Ducks play follow the leader in the middle of the ponds.

Whiskered Terns perform aerial gymnastics and Glossy Ibis stand confidently in small groups posing for the camera. White-winged Fairywrens frolic in the bushes and Black-fronted Dotterels run along the water's edge, pause, then run again. Before you object that the Black-fronted Dotterel is inappropriately named, consider that a bird's front is in fact its forehead.

A White-necked Heron stands elegantly in the shallows while Hoary-headed Grebes splash across the surface of the pond. A Buff-banded Rail, not quite so common here as the crakes, peers cautiously from behind some reeds, decides it is safe and steps tentatively into the open.

A flock of Galahs flies overhead with discordant calls and, for contrast, a Little Grassbird calls sweetly from the reeds. Out on the water, a few Australasian Shovelers are sprinkled among the

Cockatiel
Red-kneed Dotterel
Glossy Ibis
White-winged Fairywren

Pacific Black Ducks, and Grey and Chestnut Teals. Australian Shelducks stand proudly on the bank, well aware of how handsome they are.

Black Swans swim gracefully in the distance, the male's head always positioned slightly above the female's. There are some Hardheads out there too, diving under the water just as you're about to identify them. The Australasian Grebes are also diving under the water, perhaps to exasperate you, perhaps just for fun.

White-breasted Woodswallows cluster in the tree behind you, looking very smart and pristine.

Sewage treatment works usually provide great birding and Lake Cargelligo's are no exception.

White-faced Herons are very elegant birds with a heavy, slow flight.

Lake Cargelligo's sewage treatment works provide good birding. Cockatiels wheel overhead as you admire the waterfowl.

Dhilba Guuranda-Innes National Park is on the coast, 300 kilometres west of Adelaide.

69 Dhilba Guuranda-Innes National Park

Dhilba Guuranda-Innes National Park comprises 9,415 hectares of coastal vegetation on the southern tip of the Yorke Peninsula, 300 kilometres west of Adelaide. Entry and camping fees apply. The vegetation includes impenetrably dense heathlands and some regenerated mallee.

Because of the coastal location, the bird list includes quite a few seabirds, such as Flesh-footed, Short-tailed and Fluttering Shearwaters. There are also Pacific Reef Herons, and other desirable species such as Black-faced Cormorants and Hooded Plovers. Both Silver and Pacific Gulls are very common.

You would expect to see Brush Bronzewings in this habitat and indeed, like the gulls, they are very common. Common or not, I love to watch them walking with determination to get nowhere in particular. Honeyeaters are common, too, such as Red Wattlebirds, Singing and New Holland Honeyeaters. Roger loved New Holland Honeyeaters and always missed them when they

weren't about. Other honeyeaters, not quite so numerous, but nevertheless not hard to see, are Purple-gaped, Spiny-cheeked and Tawny-crowned. The dense vegetation is perfect for Silvereyes, Purple-backed Fairywrens and White-browed Scrubwren, but how Emus manage to negotiate it I am not sure. Personally, I find it extremely difficult to walk through.

But walk through it you must, if you are to pursue the most exciting bird in the national park – the White-bellied Whipbird. This bird, sometimes called the Mallee Whipbird, is paler than the Western Australian Black-throated Whipbird, and has slightly different markings on its throat. The call is quite different. The bird is supposed to sit up on a stick and sing its heart out. However, it is equally capable of skulking in the undergrowth and noiselessly and invisibly circling any birdwatching intruder.

The Grey Currawongs here are the same race that inhabits the Nullarbor – different from the ones in eastern South Australia.

Brush Bronzewing
Rock Parrot
Grey Currawong (race
  intermedia)
AND, IF YOU'RE VERY LUCKY
AND VERY PATIENT
White-bellied Whipbird

Roger's favourite honeyeater, the New Holland, is a bird with lots of personality.

Red-capped Plovers are common, as are Australian Golden Whistlers, Scarlet Robins and Southern Scrub Robins. I saw Rock Parrots, Purple-crowned Lorikeets and Tree Martins. Raptors include Nankeen Kestrels, Swamp Harriers and Collared Sparrowhawks.

Very sensibly, the Malleefowl don't live in the dense heath. They inhabit the regenerated mallee. Wouldn't you think that a bird called a Mallee Whipbird could do that too?

Dhilba Guuranda-Innes National Park is very pretty and has a good variety of birds. If you miss out on White-bellied Whipbirds, you can always enjoy the Brush Bronzewings and the New Holland Honeyeaters. You won't miss out on them.

Brush Bronzewings are common at Dhilba Guuranda-Innes National Park.

Bool Lagoon Game Reserve

'You should have been here in No-wember', said the ranger, with a thick European accent. This was many years ago, when my parents were visiting Bool Lagoon in South Australia. They were impressed with the large number of waterfowl, but the ranger felt compelled to point out that they weren't seeing the place at its best. The previous November all the swans, geese, ducks, ibis, spoonbills and Brolgas had young. It must have been quite a sight.

We visited in June 2012 and were told we were lucky that there was water in the lagoons – the place had been dry for many years. In winter, I didn't expect to see Brolgas, although the signs assured me that they'd been there in May. I did see thousands of Black Swans and overwhelming numbers of Australian Shelducks, lots of other waterbirds and several raptors. We drove to Little Bool Lagoon and saw hundreds of Eurasian Coots. What we did not see were Magpie Geese. We returned two days later in the rain and were astonished to see large numbers of Magpie Geese and not one Australian Shelduck. It was as if they had magically exchanged places. Magpie Geese became locally extinct soon after European settlement and were re-established with eggs brought from the Northern Territory.

Bool Lagoon is listed as a wetland of international significance. It is located 360 kilometres south-east of Adelaide, 23 kilometres south of Naracoorte. The site is 3,000 hectares and comprises a series of freshwater lagoons ten kilometres long. It is open all the time except on total fire ban days. Vehicle entry and camping fees apply.

There are several boardwalks and walking trails and I think I did them all. The ground was dry under the Tea-Tree Boardwalk and there were no ibis nesting in the tea-trees. I saw raptors, honeyeaters, Silvereyes and White-fronted Chats. On the Gunawar Trail, Golden-headed Cisticolas appeared on cue and Little Grassbirds made their mournful call. There were Yellow-faced Honeyeaters and Hardheads, but perhaps the Swamp Harrier had chased other birds away. On the Pat-om Walk, a pair of Black-shouldered Kites squealed at each other, ignoring me completely. The signs informed me that 'Pat-om' is the local Aboriginal word for Magpie Goose.

Red-kneed Dotterels are exceptionally handsome birds. About the last feature you notice is their red 'knees'.

Golden-headed Cisticolas like to draw attention to themselves, by sitting up high and singing loudly.

Brolga
Australian Shelduck
Magpie Goose
Golden-headed Cisticola

Bool Lagoon is a wetland of international significance with a bird list of 112 species.

Grey Fantails played around me and a large flock of Yellow-rumped Thornbills hopped among the grass. Nankeen Kestrels hovered above and Pied Stilts posed at the water's edge, admiring their own reflections.

There were ducks and dotterels, herons and honeyeaters. I enjoyed Bool Lagoon very much, but I knew I hadn't seen it at its best and vowed to return one No-wember.

What do you think is the most abundant bird in Wyperfeld National Park? Malleefowl might be the most interesting, and Splendid Fairywren might be the most gorgeous, but as to the most abundant, you might say Emu – there are lots of them and they are large and conspicuous. You could suggest Mallee Ringneck – they are both common and colourful. You might even say Spiny-cheeked Honeyeater – their loud, constant, gurgling calls draw your attention to them and make you think there are even more of them than there are. In fact, the answer is the Galah. These beautiful pink and grey characters are often overlooked because they are so familiar. This should not be so, as they are not only very pretty, but they are packed with personality.

Wyperfeld National Park is in the Victorian Mallee, 450 kilometres north-west of Melbourne. There are various ways to get there; we usually go via Rainbow. The park includes 357,000 hectares of woodlands, mallee, pine/buloke plains and dry lakebeds. In spring the wildflowers can be spectacular.

Rarely, when the Wimmera River overflows into Lake Hindmarsh and this fills Lake Albacutya, Outlet Creek fills Wyperfeld's normally dry lakes. Suddenly waterbirds arrive. As well as ducks, grebes and cormorants, there can be crakes, waders and terns.

The bird list comprises well over 200 species, with four whistlers (Rufous, Australian Golden, Red-lored and Gilbert's) and 17 honeyeaters (including White-fronted and Crimson Chats, which are classified together with the honeyeaters).

Seventeen honeyeaters is pretty special in anyone's language. After the Spiny-cheeked, the two most common are the White-eared and the Red Wattlebird. Singing are common too, as are Yellow-plumed. Then there's my favourite, the sweet little Brown-headed. Striped Honeyeaters are not common in Victoria, but you can find them at Wyperfeld. You can also find Purple-gaped, Grey-fronted and those clowns of the bird world, White-fronted. I always think of Tawny-crowned Honeyeaters as birds of coastal heath, but you can see them at Wyperfeld too.

Galahs come in for their evening drink at Wyperfeld National Park.

Tree Martins are sweet little things, most easily identified by their dirty white rumps.

Splendid Fairywren
  (race *melanotus*)
Gilbert's Whistler
Striped Honeyeater
AND, IF YOU 'RE VERY LUCKY
Red-lored Whistler

There are Major Mitchell's Cockatoos and gorgeous Spotted Pardalotes (these are the yellow-rumped race). Look for Regent Parrots walking along the branches of river red gums – instead of perching across the branch as parrots normally do. The Regents are brightly coloured, and so are Mulga Parrots, but dry country birds often exhibit subtle hues. I'm thinking of birds such as Southern Scrub Robins, Jacky Winters and Southern Whitefaces. Even Redthroats don't have a very red throat and Crested Bellbirds and Hooded Robins are both delicately sophisticated in their colouring. Horsfield's Bronze Cuckoo is another quietly understated bird, but very pretty if you look closely.

Wyperfeld has many moods. In summer, it is simply unbearably hot. At other times it can be mesmerisingly tranquil – until a flock of cockies squawks overhead to remind you who really owns the land.

The Major Mitchell's Cockatoo is a very attractive bird.

72 Round Hill Nature Reserve

Round Hill Nature Reserve is famous among birders as the spot to see Red-lored Whistlers in spring. It is an odd little patch of mallee right in the middle of New South Wales. It is about nine hours' drive from Sydney and approximately 40 kilometres north of Lake Cargelligo.

Round Hill and the adjacent Nombinnie Nature Reserve can be very hot. We were there in October 2009 and sadly, I did not see a Red-lored Whistler. I did see lots and lots of Red-capped Robins and Rufous Whistlers and millions of irritating sticky bush flies. Roger saw a snake, I saw a sand goanna and a stumpy-tailed lizard. It's that sort of country.

I saw several Shy Heathwrens and one Southern Scrub Robin. Roger did not see them. It was too hot for him; he sat in the car reading his *Financial Review*. Willie Wagtails scolded him for being such a wimp, but he didn't mind.

I persevered with the flies and the heat and was rewarded with Splendid Fairywrens and Spiny-cheeked Honeyeaters. Mulga Parrots flew overhead and I heard the beautiful rich call of the Crested Bellbird. I saw White-eared and Yellow-plumed Honeyeaters, Inland Thornbills and Weebills.

Apart from the Red-lored Whistler, other good birds I missed out on included Black Honeyeaters and Turquoise Parrots. Nor did I see Major Mitchell's Cockatoos, Rainbow Bee-eaters or Superb Parrots. On that hot October day, I did not see one raptor – although (would you believe?) both Black and Grey Falcons are on the bird list for Round Hill.

I managed to glimpse a Common Bronzewing and

Red-capped Robins are friendly, confiding little birds with a song like a telephone ringing.

several Mallee Ringnecks. Aren't they a gorgeous colour? I never tire of watching them, and when they're a distraction from the flies, they are doubly welcome.

Grey-fronted Honeyeaters are common at Round Hill, as are White-fronted, Striped and (my favourite) Brown-headed. There are Speckled Warblers and Spotted Bowerbirds, Western Gerygones and Southern Whitefaces. If you see babblers, they're probably White-browed, although Grey-crowned are also on the list. Both Masked and White-browed Woodswallows are here, along with Chestnut Quail-thrush.

Both Australian Owlet and Spotted Nightjars are a possibility, the latter most likely to be seen on the road at night.

Round Hill is an interesting spot. Sadly, spring seems to be the only time you're likely to see Red-lored Whistlers and, as Roger would readily have confirmed, conditions may not be comfortable at that time of year.

Red-capped Robin
Southern Scrub Robin
Shy Heathwren
AND, IF YOU'RE VERY LUCKY
Red-lored Whistler

Round Hill Nature Reserve is a small patch of mallee, nine hours' drive from Sydney.

Spotted Nightjars are most likely to be seen on the road at night.

From the air, you get a hint of the isolation of the West MacDonnell Ranges.

Tjoritja/West MacDonnell National Park

73

Spinifex Pigeons must be the funniest birds in Tjoritja/ West MacDonnell National Park. With their spiky hairdo and their flawless cinnamon plumage, they run from here to there with exaggerated self-importance. And then they run back again. I love them.

If Spinifex Pigeons are the funniest, Dusky Grasswren must be the most sought after. Then, perhaps, come Western Bowerbirds and Black-breasted Buzzards.

Tjoritja/West MacDonnell National Park, west of Alice Springs in the Northern Territory, is renowned for spectacular scenery. The park is huge (250 kilometres long!) and incorporates many tourist attractions, such as King's Canyon, Palm Valley, Simpson's Gap, Standley Chasm and Ormiston Gorge.

Spinifex Pigeons are the clowns of Tjoritja/West MacDonnell National Park.

I saw my first Dusky Grasswren at King's Canyon. They were running around under foot like little mice. These surely must be the easiest grasswren of all to tick. I saw my first Black-breasted Buzzard here too, with his great big white bull's-eyes on his underwings.

I grew up believing that Western and Spotted Bowerbirds were conspecific and was delighted when ornithologists finally woke up to themselves and agreed that the two species were distinct – a fact that John Gould had known since the 19th century. To be fair, they do look alike. I saw my first Western Bowerbird at Ormiston Gorge, where this photo was taken – not by me, I hasten to add, but by my mate Mick Roderick.

Ormiston Gorge is also home to elusive Rufous-crowned Emu-wrens. These delicate little birds, with their bright blue faces and elegant erect tails, are always exciting to see. There are fairywrens here too: Splendid and Purple-backed and White-winged.

There are Peregrine Falcons in the MacDonnell Ranges, and just a remote chance of a Grey Falcon.

Along with the hilarious Spinifex Pigeons, there are Crested Pigeons, and Diamond and Peaceful Doves.

Flocks of budgies are common, as are Port Lincoln Parrots, with their striking black heads. Officially classified as a race of the Australian Ringneck, these parrots look quite different from Mallee Ringnecks and occupy quite different habitat from the south-west's Twenty-eight Parrot. Yet, together with the Cloncurry Parrot, we're told that they're all Australian Ringnecks.

Red-backed Kingfishers like this dry country, as do Pied Butcherbirds, and of course the most common woodswallow is the Black-faced. There are 17 honeyeaters, including Crimson and Orange Chats. The most common honeyeater is the White-plumed, followed by Yellow-throated Miner, Spiny-cheeked, Singing, Brown and Grey-headed Honeyeater.

Tjoritja/West MacDonnell National Park has been nominated for World Heritage status. It is an iconic part of the continent that every Australian really should see. And I guarantee you'll fall in love with the Spinifex Pigeons.

It's great to see the lilac nuchal crest as this Western Bowerbird feeds its young.

Dusky Grasswren
Western Bowerbird
Black-breasted Buzzard
Spinifex Pigeon

The mighty Murchison River carves its way through Kalbarri National Park.

74

Kalbarri National Park

Six hundred and forty-four kilometres north of Perth in Western Australia, the mighty Murchison River carves its way through multicoloured rocks. Kalbarri National Park embraces this gorge and altogether encompasses 183,000 hectares of pretty beaches with rugged cliffs, dramatic river gorges and extensive sand plains. The park boasts over 1,000 species of wildflower, including banksias, grevilleas, hibiscus, kangaroo paw and verticordia.

When I was there 40 years ago, I paid 20 cents to put on earphones and hear recordings of birds in the park. I heard a Bush Stone-curlew, a Willie Wagtail, a Grey Shrikethrush, a Rufous Whistler, a Crested Bellbird and a Brown Honeyeater. Birders wouldn't pay 20 cents for that today: they all have free apps on their mobile phones.

Pacific Gulls do not confine themselves to the Pacific coast. They are found here too, living contentedly on the Indian Ocean.

In a park that prides itself on its spectacular wildflowers, it is only appropriate that honeyeaters take pride of place on the bird list. Brown, Singing and White-cheeked are very common. Spiny-cheeked are numerous, as are White-fronted Chats. Less plentiful are Pied, White-fronted, Tawny-crowned, my old friends White-plumed, and Crimson Chats. Not a bad list.

Visitors to Kalbarri are also spoiled for choice when it comes to fairywrens. There are no fewer than four species in the park. Purple-backed are the most common, followed by Splendid – and splendid indeed they are. White-winged are by no means rare; nor are Blue-breasted, come to that.

Brown Honeyeater
Purple-backed Fairywren
Australian Pipit
White-backed Swallow

Australian Pelicans, Silver Gulls and Galahs vie with each other to be the most numerous bird in the park. Close behind are Pacific Gulls and Willie Wagtails. I saw a Wedge-tailed Eagle, Red-capped Plovers and Greater Crested Terns. Magpie-larks were plentiful, but I missed magpies. There are Emus on the plains and Australasian Gannets out at sea.

It is disappointing to note that exotic Laughing Doves are now well established here. I didn't see any 40 years ago. Of course, there are Crested Pigeons too. I do love these self-important birds with their pretty pink feet. Let's face it, I love any bird with a crest: such an unnecessary, self-indulgent adornment.

The most common raptor is the Nankeen Kestrel, followed by the Little Eagle. Ospreys are common too, and there's always a chance of a Black-breasted Buzzard or a Peregrine Falcon.

You'll probably see Port Lincoln Parrots and Caspian Terns, Silvereyes, Tree Martins and Australian Pipits. You'll certainly see Australian Ravens, White-backed Swallows and Zebra Finches.

Kalbarri is a very rugged part of the world. The birding is good and the locals boast that the weather is always perfect.

The Brown Honeyeater has a wide distribution and a loud, warbling call

75

Lake Bindegolly National Park

After heavy rain, Lake Bindegolly in south-west Queensland can attract thousands of waterbirds.

A birding friend of mine saw a Grey Falcon at Lake Bindegolly. I didn't. Nor did I see any Freckled Ducks which, by all accounts, are seen frequently. In fact, I didn't see any ducks at all.

Lake Bindegolly National Park is located 40 kilometres east of Thargomindah (or 145 kilometres west of Cunnamulla) in south-west Queensland. It is on the Bulloo Developmental Road, which tourist promoters like to dub 'Adventure Way'. While the park is called Lake Bindegolly National Park, there are several lakes here: Lakes Bindegolly and Toomaroo are saline and Lake Hutchinson is freshwater. After heavy rain, they join together to form one large wetland and can attract thousands of waterbirds.

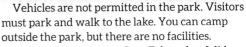

Remember that a bird's front is its forehead, and you won't think that the Black-fronted Dotterel is inappropriately named.

Vehicles are not permitted in the park. Visitors must park and walk to the lake. You can camp outside the park, but there are no facilities.

I may not have seen a Grey Falcon, but I did see a Black one. He was sitting on the ground, jet black against the red earth, with a light blue bill. I also saw Whistling Kites and a Brown Goshawk. I may not have seen any ducks, but I saw several waterbirds. I remember pelicans, cormorants and spoonbills, Great Egrets and sundry White-faced Herons. Black-fronted Dotterels ran their twinkling run at the edge of the water. I also remember purple eremophila and legions of lizards.

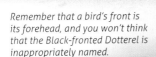

I saw several Australian Pratincole sitting on the red earth pretending to be invisible. Once I'd picked one out, I saw more and more.

There were Crested Pigeons and Diamond Doves. White-backed Swallows swooped overhead, as well as Fairy Martins.

One lone Black-faced Cuckooshrike landed on a branch and shuffled his wings, and a Magpie-lark raised his wings and told his wife: 'Pee wee!' She agreed categorically, 'Pee wee', and lifted her wings too, to emphasise the point.

On the ground I saw White-winged Fairywren, Southern Whiteface and many Zebra Finches. One Pied Butcherbird looked immaculate in his black and white beauty.

Flocks of budgies and Cockatiels wheeled overhead, Mallee Ringnecks whooshed past with a flash of vibrant green, and a pair of Bourke's Parrots sat quietly watching me. Eastern Bluebonnets were common – I wish now that I'd counted how many I saw.

The Spiny-cheeked Honeyeater was probably the most abundant species. I was constantly aware of them: when I couldn't see them I could hear them, either warbling happily or reprimanding each other with a sharp 'chock!' I saw Crimson Chats and Yellow-throated Miners.

A Grey Falcon would have been most welcome, but I didn't go hungry, did I?

Black-faced Woodswallow
Diamond Dove
Black-fronted Dotterel
Zebra Finch

I did not see a Grey Falcon at Lake Bindegolly, but I'm told that others have.

Deane Lewis <www.dl.id.au>

The Varied Lorikeet is a small green parrot found only in the northern tropics.

76

Adelaide River Crossing

When you're travelling between Darwin and Kakadu, it's worth pausing where the Arnhem Highway crosses the Adelaide River to look for Mangrove Golden Whistlers and Arafura Fantails.

In 2009 when we travelled from Darwin to Kakadu, we stopped at the Adelaide River Crossing on our way there and on our way back. Both visits were very short and we didn't walk far. We simply poked about in the mangroves. On both occasions we saw an Arafura Fantail and a Mangrove Golden Whistler, once a female, once a male. Little wonder the Adelaide River Crossing gets into my top 100 sites.

Everyone remembers the hilarious jumping crocodile at the Adelaide River Crossing. But perhaps not everyone approves of tourist operators who think making crocodiles jump out of the water for a free feed is entertaining.

The Adelaide River Crossing is on the Stuart Highway about 110 kilometres south of Darwin. Mangroves beside the river provide a home for fantails, flycatchers and gerygones, and the river means waterbirds also feature on the bird list. You can see Magpie Geese, Radjah Shelduck, Black-necked Stork, and both Pied and Striated Herons. There are even Brolgas on the list. Other good birds that have been seen here include Pheasant Coucals, Spangled Drongos and Zitting Cisticolas.

The first time we stopped, we spent 20 minutes looking for a male Mangrove Golden Whistler. We saw a female almost immediately and noted her yellow underparts. Then we spied an Arafura Fantail darting about in the mangroves. He was very different from the Rufous Fantail I'm familiar with, making me wonder why it took ornithologists so long to recognize him as a separate species.

In those 20 minutes we saw a Mistletoebird, a Large-billed Gerygone, a Blue-faced Honeyeater, and both Shining and Leaden Flycatchers. (Broad-billed and Paperbark Flycatchers are also on the list, but we didn't see them.) We saw three raptors (wedgie, Whistling and Black-shouldered Kites), Sulphur-crested Cockatoos and Varied Lorikeets. But alas, there was no male Mangrove Golden Whistler. The female was very pretty and we had no right to be disappointed at not seeing a male. But of course we were.

Five days later, on our return to Darwin, we stopped at the crocodile clown again. Straightaway we saw a glorious male Mangrove Golden Whistler, then another Arafura Fantail. We saw none of the other birds we'd seen on our previous visit. Instead, we saw a Little Bronze Cuckoo, a Brown Honeyeater and a Varied Triller.

You may not approve of hand feeding crocodiles as a tourist attraction, but you will certainly enjoy a few minutes birding in the mangroves at the Adelaide River Crossing.

This local landmark shows you where to look for Mangrove Golden Whistlers and Arafura Fantails.

Hyperactive Arafura Fantails demand the birder's attention at Adelaide River Crossing.

 Mangrove Golden Whistler
Arafura Fantail
Shining Flycatcher
Leaden Flycatcher

77

Rinyirru (Lakefield) National Park

Many birders visit Rinyirru or Lakefield National Park hoping for a Red Goshawk. I went there hoping for a Star Finch and a Red-chested Buttonquail. I wasn't disappointed.

At over 5,000 square kilometres, Lakefield is Queensland's second largest national park. It is located in the middle of Cape York and it takes about six hours to drive here from Cairns. Being so large, it incorporates several different habitats: mangroves and mudflats, grassy plains, sandstone escarpments and huge rivers that contract to permanent waterholes during the dry season. Any one of these waterholes can be home to a crocodile or perhaps a Comb-crested Jacana.

Located in the north of the park, Nifold Plain is a huge flat grassy plain studded with termite mounds. There is not a tree in sight, which makes the Brolgas and the bustards stand out. Emus would look right at home wandering across these grasslands, but

Flat, grassy, Nifold Plain is just one of the varied habitats in Lakefield National Park.

they are not common here. This is where I saw my first Star Finch, sitting by himself on a rock. This, the Cape York race, is in decline and its range is contracting. Other finches at Lakefield include Black-throated, Crimson and Masked, as well as Chestnut-breasted Mannikins.

We saw Jacky Winters, Willie Wagtails and Magpie-larks. A Spotted Harrier flew low above the grass. Lakefield is quite a good venue for raptors with 19 on the list, including the rare and endangered Red Goshawk. The most common bird of prey by far is the Whistling Kite.

We found a pleasant waterhole where we ate our lunch, having a good look around for crocodiles before we sat down. Here we saw Rufous-banded Honeyeaters, a Rufous Whistler and a Nankeen Night Heron.

In order to distribute their weight evenly across the lilypads, Comb-crested Jacanas have unbelievably huge feet.

Rainbow Bee-eaters entertained us, Red-backed Fairywrens played nearby and a White-throated Gerygone tinkled his delightful song down the scale.

The only corvids are Torresian Crows, which makes identification easy. There are Green Orioles, Spangled Drongos and Fairy Gerygones, Blue-winged Kookaburras and Red-tailed Black Cockatoos. Golden-shouldered Parrots are on the list too, but they are seen more reliably at nearby Musgrave Station.

At night we went spotlighting and saw Spotted Nightjars, Papuan Frogmouth and Bush Stone-curlews (with those huge eyes they simply have to be nocturnal). And, I'm delighted to say, we also saw Red-chested Buttonquail. I knew they were small birds, but this little fellow caught in our spotlight beam looked pathetically tiny. These birds are widespread and common, but I'd never seen one and I was tickled pink to rectify the omission.

I recommend Lakefield, but only during the dry season, from April to October. It is remote, harsh country, but it is the only place I know to see the Cape York Star Finch.

Australian Bustards stand out on the treeless plains in Lakefield National Park.

Australian Bustard
Red-chested Buttonquail
Star Finch (race *clarenscens*)
AND, IF YOU'RE LUCKY
Red Goshawk

78

White-quilled Rock Pigeons have a limited range, but are locally common.

Mitchell Plateau

Australian birders have always visited the Mitchell Falls for the Black Grasswren. Since the Kimberley Honeyeater has been split from the White-lined, birders now have two special reasons to visit. In fact, there are many reasons to come here.

Located in the far north of the rugged remote Kimberley, the Mitchell Plateau cannot be accessed by standard 2WD. Conventional wisdom is that you need 4WD because of all the deep creek crossings. We flew in by helicopter. From our base in Kununurra, we flew to the Mitchell Plateau in a Piper Cherokee. It took 65 minutes. Then a short helicopter ride took us to the falls.

The first birds we saw as we landed were a Magpie-lark, a Black-faced Cuckooshrike and a Peaceful Dove. Then a raptor provoked discussion: was it an Australian Hobby? After due consideration, we agreed it was a Peregrine Falcon. We walked to Little Merton Falls, seeing a Brush Cuckoo and a Kimberley Honeyeater along the way. How easy was that? Then we glimpsed Black Grasswren, chased after them and eventually had most satisfying views. These are the biggest grasswren. They sit up straight and proud, as if they're aware how special and how beautiful they are.

We also saw White-quilled Rock Pigeons, Purple-backed Fairywren and Great Bowerbirds. We were disappointed on missing out on the Kimberley race of Partridge Pigeons – the ones with yellow faces. We were told that they came in to drink every morning at a water container outside the helicopter flight office. That is, every morning

Black Grasswren
Kimberley Honeyeater
Partridge Pigeon (race *blaauwi*)
White-quilled Rock Pigeon

except the morning we were there. To make up for this disappointment, we saw a narbalek, a cute little wallaby with a grey bushy tail.

We saw Weebill, Mistletoebirds and Double-barred Finches. Red-winged Parrots flew over, as did Torresian Crows, and Sulphur-crested Cockatoos squawked at us rudely. Rainbow Bee-eaters were showing off as usual and we saw Silver-crowned Friarbirds and both Rufous-throated and White-gaped Honeyeaters. There were White-winged Trillers and Striated Pardalotes. As we were about to leave, a Whistling Kite flew over. We left at 10.30 am, both pleased and relieved that we'd seen our two target species.

If you go to the Mitchell Plateau, you are guaranteed to see a Pied Butcherbird, a Red-tailed Black Cockatoo, and both Brown and Bar-breasted Honeyeaters. Unfortunately, you are not guaranteed to see a Black Grasswren or a Kimberley Honeyeater. Or the Kimberley race of the Partridge Pigeon.

Our largest grasswren, the Black, sits up proud and tall as if he knows he's special.

The Mitchell Falls provide a welcome splash of coolness in the hot Kimberley.

79

Rutherglen

You can see why Zebra Finches are such popular cage birds: they really are very attractive.

The ephemeral swamp near the Rutherglen tip can be very productive.

We were scheduled to leave for a few days in Rutherglen, when I received a newsletter from one of the wineries. 'Greetings from soggy Rutherglen', it began. I shrugged and resigned myself to getting wet feet. In Rutherglen, some things you can do from the car and some things you must do on foot.

For example, you must walk around Lake King. This lake beside the caravan park is always worth exploring. Rutherglen is the only place in Victoria I know where I can get White-breasted Woodswallows. In summer they cluster high up in the river red gums in the caravan park. There are other summer migrants too. There's often a Rufous Songlark sitting on some high perch singing his distinctive song as if his life depended on it. Australian Reed Warblers nest in the reeds at the western end of the lake and Sacred Kingfishers perch on nearby electricity wires. At any time of year I see Black-fronted Dotterels, Yellow Rosellas and darters, and there are always ducks and coots and moorhens. There's an island in the lake where large flocks of ibis (both Australian White and Straw-necked) roost, decorating the one

My favourite woodswallow, the White-breasted, is difficult to find in Victoria. But each summer I see it in Rutherglen in the state's north.

large gumtree like Christmas ornaments. Nankeen Night Herons sometimes roost here too and once I saw 40 Masked Lapwings loafing on the island's muddy bank. Huge flocks of Galahs and Sulphur-crested Cockatoos can be a noisy distraction, and Australasian Swamphen strut haughtily from the lake to the adjoining golf course. Little Friarbirds feed in the grevilleas along the northern bank.

On that particular soggy trip, I saw many families of Australasian Grebe – I wish now that I'd counted them. It must have been a good year for them. The parents always managed to see me before I saw them and called loudly to their stripy-headed youngsters, instructing them to escape from the bad birder. 'Kek-kek-kek!' squawked the parents with loud urgency. Unlike human children, the little grebelings rushed to obey.

Along the main street, I always inspect all the sparrows, hoping to spot a Eurasian Tree Sparrow, while Blue-faced Honeyeaters fly overhead. In the grassy paddocks on the edge of town, I look for Zebra Finch and Stubble Quail. In summer, I hope for Red-backed Kingfishers.

Rutherglen's best birding spot is as fickle as the weather. Sometimes it provides breathtaking birding; sometimes it is an unremarkable cow paddock. It's on the road to Chiltern near the turnoff

White-breasted Woodswallow
Zebra Finch
Blue-faced Honeyeater
AND, IF YOU'RE LUCKY
Turquoise Parrot

to the tip. When there's water lying around, you must stop for a look. Sit in your car and count how many species you can see. There are snipe and swallows, ducks and dotterels, cormorants and crakes. I've seen White-breasted Woodswallows here too, and Turquoise Parrots, White-backed Swallows, Diamond Firetails, and Tree and Fairy Martins. One year an Australian Painted-snipe reared his chicks in this swamp and birders drove up from Melbourne to admire him. He's not as colourful as his missus, but his cute fluffy chicks were certainly worth the drive.

But, to be honest, I think that Rutherglen is always worth the drive. Apart from the birds, there are always the wineries.

Our most gorgeous finch, the Gouldian, is no longer classified as endangered and can be seen around Katherine.

Black-faced Woodswallows have a very wide distribution, but seem to prefer drier, hotter country.

80

Katherine

I first visited Katherine in 1982. I loved it then and I love it now. Of course, it helps that my father was stationed there during the Second World War and liked it so much he named me 'Susan Katherine'.

On that first visit, I noted in my diary that the weather was perfect, although it was hot overnight. I photographed the bower of a Great Bowerbird, did a cruise up the gorge and saw peregrines nesting high up on the sandstone cliffs. I made an unsuccessful search for bustards, but did manage to see Blue-faced Honeyeaters, Oriental Dollarbirds, Black Kites, Magpie-larks and Shining Flycatchers. I also saw Pallid Cuckoos, Rainbow Bee-eaters, Brown Honeyeaters and Red-collared Lorikeets. I admired bright blue water lilies, and noted that most of the vegetation was savanna woodland with small patches of isolated monsoon rainforest.

Katherine is 320 kilometres (or about three hours' drive) south-east of Darwin on the Stuart Highway. The population is around 6,000. Birders visit Edith

Falls Road, north of Katherine, to look for Hooded Parrots and Gouldian Finches, and the Katherine Gorge in Nitmiluk National Park for Great-billed Heron and Red Goshawk.

On my most recent trip to Katherine, I'm delighted to say that I did see both Hooded Parrots and Gouldian Finches on the Edith Falls Road. There were about 40 Gouldians, mainly young birds, but including several spectacular red-heads and at least two black-heads. Not long ago, we feared for the future of these gorgeous finches. Today, the population decline has ceased and the species is no longer listed as endangered. This success is put down to proper fire management.

We also saw about 50 Long-tailed Finches – a wonderful sight. There were also Red-backed Kingfishers, Black-faced Woodswallows and Diamond Doves. We saw those most appropriately named birds, Varied Sittellas. These birds vary enormously as you travel around the continent, always leaving me bemused as to whether they're really all the same species. The day started with early flocks of Cockatiels, Galahs and Red-tailed Black Cockatoos, and ended with clouds of thousands of black flying-foxes.

We also managed to flush a small covey of Chestnut-backed Buttonquail in the vicinity of the road to Chinamans Creek. This was off the Victoria Highway, about 15 kilometres south of Katherine.

At Mataranka, about 100 kilometres south of Katherine, we saw Red Goshawks, along with Red-winged Parrots, Budgerigars and Masked Finches.

There's a lot to see around Katherine, including some very special, very colourful birds.

Nitmiluk Gorge in Katherine is picturesque and popular.

Gouldian Finch
Hooded Parrot
Long-tailed Finch
AND, IF YOU'RE LUCKY
Chestnut-backed Buttonquail

81

There are 19 species of honeyeater at Abattoir Swamp, including the White-cheeked.

Abattoir Swamp

What immediately comes to mind when I ponder Abattoir Swamp is not the swamp at all. It is Red-winged Parrots flying through the trees, honeyeaters in the car park, and Brown Quail scurrying to hide underneath the boardwalk on the way to the bird hide. When I was there last, the melaleucas were flowering and Yellow, White-throated and Lewin's Honeyeaters were making the most of it.

Abattoir Swamp Environmental Park gives its address as Julatten and is located on the Mossman to Mount Molloy Road in far north Queensland. It can call itself an environmental park as much as it likes, it will never live down its most unfortunate moniker.

This is reputedly a good spot for crakes, although I've never been lucky enough to see one here. Other people have and there are three on the list,

as well as Pale-vented Bush-hens and Buff-banded Rails. The three crakes are White-browed, Spotless and Baillon's.

Although it's a swamp, it is sometimes dry. This doesn't matter, as the bush birds are just as interesting as the waterbirds. The good thing about a dry swamp is you don't need any insect repellant. Red-backed Fairywrens hop about in the car park, and Rainbow Bee-eaters fly overhead making their metallic trill. You can see Leaden Flycatchers and Northern Fantails. There are Grey Fantails here too and they dart

With or without water, Abattoir Swamp can provide very good birding.

172

about constantly, while the Northern ones sit quietly erect with true military discipline.

If you see a cuckooshrike here, it's more likely to be White-bellied than Black-faced. They always look exceptionally clean to me. Gorgeous Forest Kingfishers sit quietly watching you, while Mistletoebirds call loudly from the canopy.

There are both Olive-backed Orioles and Olive-backed Sunbirds, and both Peaceful and Bar-shouldered Doves. Rufous Whistlers draw attention to themselves with their loud 'E-chong!' and Australasian Figbirds are often seen, as are Rufous Shrikethrushes.

The most common honeyeater is the Brown. Then comes the Yellow, White-throated, Brown-backed and Yellow-faced. There are a remarkable 19 species of honeyeater on the bird list, although some, like the Helmeted Friarbird, are seen rarely. Dusky and Scarlet Myzomelas, and Blue-faced Honeyeaters are much more likely to be present, and watch out for White-cheeked.

When there's water in the swamp, there are ducks, egrets, herons and cormorants. Masked Lapwings stand idly by, always looking as if they're up to no good. There might be a darter or a Black-necked Stork. There could be jacana or Australasian Grebes.

Notwithstanding its bloody appellation, Abattoir Swamp can provide very good birding. When the melaleucas are flowering, there is no need to leave the car park.

Gorgeous Red-winged Parrots are often seen in the car park at Abattoir Swamp.

Red-winged Parrot
Brown Quail
Forest Kingfisher
Chestnut-breasted Mannikin

82

Lake Joondalup (Yellagonga Regional Park)

The Crested Honey Buzzard flew right over my head.

Birders know Lake Joondalup because every summer for the last few years a Crested Honey Buzzard has turned up here. Also known as the Oriental Honey Buzzard, this exotic bird, vagrant to Australia, breeds in Siberia and Japan and migrates to Asia. A few fly off course and visit Australia.

Lake Joondalup is half an hour's drive north of Perth and is well worth a visit even if you don't want to see a Crested Honey Buzzard. It's an easy 16-kilometre walk around the lake with plenty of birds to admire. Lake Joondalup is within Yellagonga Regional Park, designated as an Important Bird Area because it provides habitat for endangered Carnaby's Black Cockatoos.

I visited in November 2018 and was alarmed by the number of enormous, hungry ticks. They were the size of one cent coins (remember them?). I also saw a beautiful little shiny bronze skink, and lots of dog walkers, but no buzzard. I'd been told the buzzard put in an appearance each morning between 9 and 10 am. I arrived just after 6 and left, disappointed, at 10.30.

Not to be discouraged so easily, I was back next morning, just after 7. It was quite warm. I stood in the shade looking west, from whence the buzzards were supposed to come. I'd seen Swamp Harriers and Whistling Kites. A distant Square-tailed Kite made my heart leap momentarily, until I satisfied myself as to its identity. I'm usually pleased to see

Lake Joondalup is a large expanse of water, accommodating many waterbirds.

these raptors, but not today. Then a Little Eagle put in an appearance. I figured I was going to see every Western Australian raptor – except a Crested Honey Buzzard. But, at 9 am, right on cue, two honey buzzards flew towards me, then right over my head, giving excellent views. No wonder I like Lake Joondalup!

Having got my quarry, I had time to relax and enjoy the walk. My notebook records 52 species for the morning, mainly waterbirds, but also bush birds and, of course, raptors. When I saw a Brown Goshawk, I had an impressive six species of raptor on my list. I saw Rainbow Bee-eaters, Rufous Whistlers and Western Gerygones. I saw Inland Thornbills, Spotted Scrubwren and Weebills. I saw Sacred Kingfishers, Musk Ducks and Nankeen Night Herons. I saw Blue-billed Duck (always a thrill!), all three grebes and Buff-banded Rail.

I did not see Carnaby's Black Cockatoo. But I saw some wonderful birds, including a Crested Honey Buzzard, and I managed to avoid the voracious ticks.

Carnaby's Black Cockatoo
Blue-billed Duck
Western Gerygone
AND A SPECIAL ONE TO FIND
Crested Honey Buzzard
(summer)

The Spotted Scrubwren, that we used to call the western race of the White-browed Scrubwren, now has species status.

83

Wilsons Promontory National Park

My girlfriend describes the call of the Little Wattlebird as a cross between the quack of a duck and the noise of a squeaky gate.

Yellow-tailed Black Cockatoo
Pacific Gull
AND, IF YOU'RE LUCKY
Hooded Plover
Beautiful Firetail

Beautiful Firetails hop among the dense coastal heaths and White-bellied Sea Eagles soar on the thermals above. The sea is blue; the sand is white. Huge brown and orange granite boulders shelter little private coves where Hooded Plovers run safely on the beach. Emus roam the plains and Little Wattlebirds squawk in the banksias.

Wilsons Promontory National Park is the southernmost tip of the Australian mainland. Known affectionately as 'The Prom', the park is located 250 kilometres south-east of Melbourne via the South Gippsland Highway. Tidal River is one of Australia's best beaches. The park is popular for bushwalking, camping, stunning wildflowers and spectacular views. More importantly, it's a good spot for Forest Ravens, and hard work and good luck could possibly produce Eastern Ground Parrots.

Out to sea you may see Australasian Gannets plunge-diving or Caspian Terns flying overhead. You might even see some Little Penguins swimming. Here Pacific Gulls are as common as Silver Gulls. On the rocks you will see Black-faced Cormorants. On the beaches there are Sooty Oystercatchers or perhaps Cape Barren Geese. Chestnut Teal and Pacific Black Duck swim in the river and White-faced Herons survey the shallows. A flock of Gang-gang Cockatoos flies by, making soft creaking screeches. A Swamp Harrier flies low, looking for easy prey. Buff-banded Rail take cover in the reeds, while Australasian Swamphens strut about with confidence. Pairs of Masked Lapwings have a proprietary air; if you forget who's boss, they'll soon remind you.

You hear the wail of Yellow-tailed Black Cockatoos and look up to see the flock fly overhead. They are big, beautiful birds and it's always a thrill to see them. They're quite common at The Prom.

Crimson Rosellas are common too, but nonetheless handsome in their royal blue and vivid red livery. Laughing Kookaburras chortle and inquisitive Grey Fantails approach you to make friends. Welcome Swallows follow you swooping at the insects you disturb, and Eastern Yellow Robins sit quietly, watching your every move. You hear the rich, fluting song of the Grey Shrikethrush and the whip-crack call of the Eastern Whipbird. You'll see Bassian Thrush hopping in the shadows and

The Prom, located 250 kilometres from Melbourne, has a bird list of 250 species.

White-throated Treecreepers creeping up the trunks of trees. You might see an Olive Whistler or a Satin Flycatcher, or perhaps a Rose or a Pink Robin.

Wilsons Promontory National Park has much to offer. With a bird list containing an impressive 250 species, you won't go home disappointed.

Dressed in red and royal blue, Crimson Rosellas are very colourful parrots, too often taken for granted.

84

Cootamundra

Sporting fans may think of Cootamundra as Don Bradman's birthplace, gardeners probably view it as the home of the Cootamundra Wattle, but I regard it as a pleasant birding spot and, in particular, a good place to see Superb Parrots.

I'll never forget sitting at a picnic table in Albert Park in Cootamundra, innocently eating my lunch and suddenly becoming aware that there were lots of parrots roosting quietly in the large deciduous trees overhead. I put down my sandwich and inspected the birds. They were Superb Parrots. And superb they were, both in name and in appearance. It's always satisfying to set out to find a particular bird, then, after some work, to succeed with unambiguous sightings. But I sometimes think that it's even better to happen across a species unexpectedly, as I did that day in Albert Park.

Once, driving to Cootamundra along Olympic Way, we encountered a plague of locusts. A spectacularly large number of White-browed Woodswallows was feasting on them. However, I've never seen either locusts or woodswallows on this section of road since.

But there are several spots around Cootamundra where you can reliably see good birds. Right in the township, in the early morning, just before dawn, Galahs and Blue-faced Honeyeaters compete to be the first bird of the day. Pioneer Park is a good spot for Common Bronzewing; Jindalee State Forest has lots of honeyeaters and treecreepers; Stockinbingal is home to Varied Sittella, White-winged Chough and White-browed Babblers. A brochure available at the Information Centre also recommends the golf course, Bland Creek and Wallendoon Lane. If you have plenty of

A Brown Falcon surveys the countryside at Cootamundra.

Superb Parrots are appropriately named.

Superb Parrot
Western Gerygone
Pied Butcherbird
Yellow-tufted Honeyeater

Sue Taylor

time, it would be worth visiting them all. However, if your time is limited there is one spot you should not miss.

It is Migurra Walk, located south of Cootamundra on the Olympic Way, about 15 kilometres from town. The walk takes you through remnant eucalypt woodland, and the birding is great. The good folk of Cootamundra, being especially proud of their wattles, inform us that there are no fewer than 22 species of acacia in the reserve. It is also a wonderful spot for arachnologists – there are

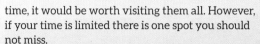

squillions of spiders: spectacular golden orbs, several leaf-curling experts and lots of different bird-dropping spiders. They all like to construct their webs across the walking track. Naturally.

Apart from Superb Parrots, at Migurra Walk I've seen Common Bronzewings, Western Gerygones, honeyeaters, thornbills, pardalotes and, once, a Painted Buttonquail. Last time I was there, a Pied Butcher-bird sat atop a dead tree and serenaded me for a glorious half an hour. Sometimes the Yellow-tufted Honeyeaters dominate, but who could whinge about an abundance of such a beautiful bird?

Without hesitation, I recommend Migurra Walk. It's only 750 metres long and you can do it quite quickly, if the spiders let you.

Blue-faced Honeyeaters vie with Galahs to be the first bird of the day.

85

Cowra

Cowra is four hours' drive west of Sydney in central west New South Wales. If you call into the Cowra Information Centre, you can watch the hologram about the Japanese prisoner-of-war breakout in 1944, and you can pick up a brochure giving you a local bird list and detailed directions about how to get to all the best birding spots.

Much of the land around Cowra is used for agriculture, but there is untouched remnant bush in Rosenberg and Neville State Forests, and good birding also along Back Creek Travelling Stock Reserve and the Wyangala State Recreation Area. There are lots of good bush birds, such as Black-chinned Honeyeaters and Restless Flycatchers.

On one occasion, as Rog and I drove into Cowra, we happened to see a signpost to Koorawatha Falls and thought we'd take a look. The dirt road was a bit bumpy, but we were well rewarded with Varied Sittellas, Spotted Pardalotes and Double-barred Finches. Amiable Grey Fantails entertained us with their tireless dancing, while Sacred Kingfishers sat motionless and unimpressed. As usual, we heard the unmistakable tinkling call of the White-throated Gerygone before we saw him high in a eucalypt, his bright yellow underparts conspicuous among the grey-green gum leaves. Nearer to ground level, a feisty Willie Wagtail was attacking a young Pallid Cuckoo. How did he know it would grow into a parasite?

While Roger read his newspaper, I tried to identify the strange bird making melodious fluty calls. He was sitting up very high in the top of a gum tree, obscured by a branch, making a rich, tuneful sound I'd never heard before. My neck was sore from craning into the canopy, but eventually I saw him. It was a Noisy Friarbird, extending his normal repertoire, more than making up for any perceived lack of comeliness with his angelic voice.

The next morning, we visited the Common before breakfast. I don't know why I think of commons as flat grasslands. The Cowra Common is a prominent rocky ridge with huge granite boulders and white box woodland. I remember Eastern Rosellas, Eastern Yellow Robins and a Peregrine Falcon.

We had breakfast in the Japanese Garden Cafe while a Blue-faced Honeyeater ate persimmons in the tree above our heads.

Then we drove to the Morongla cemetery, where Apostlebirds appeared right on cue. We looked for Grey-crowned Babblers in the adjacent bush and saw instead Western Gerygone. In summer, this is a good spot for Superb Parrot.

Cowra gave me good birding. Anywhere I see a Speckled Warbler is all right with me and I came away with a commendable six species of thornbill (Yellow, Yellow-rumped, Chestnut-rumped, Buff-rumped, Inland and Brown). And the bird list promises other treasures, like Australasian Bittern, Square-tailed Kite, Little Buttonquail and Swift Parrot. Quite a spot, Cowra.

A Noisy Friarbird confused me with his unusual call for quite some time.

Grey Fantails are very
common and very
confiding.

Noisy Friarbird
White-throated Gerygone
Black-chinned Honeyeater
Peregrine Falcon

The road into Koorawatha
Falls near Cowra was bad,
but the birds were good.

In one day's birding in summer in Royal National Park it is easy to clock up over 100 species. That's pretty good. And they're good birds, too. Birds like Superb Lyrebirds, Beautiful Firetails, Southern Emu-wrens, Tawny-crowned Honeyeaters and Scarlet Myzomelas.

Royal is Australia's oldest national park, proclaimed in 1879, an astounding 22 years before the Commonwealth of Australia was founded. Located 31 kilometres south of Sydney, the park provides 16,000 hectares of wonderful wilderness. It comprises a variety of habitats accommodating a variety of birds. There are tall open forest, heathland, rainforest, sandstone gullies, wetlands, including mangroves and mudflats, rivers and the ocean.

Powerful Owls are common in the park, Greater Sooty Owls less so. Silvereyes are abundant and widespread. Chestnut-rumped Heathwren are very common, but alas, hard to see. Pilotbirds take some patience, but they are there. Critically endangered Swift Parrots sometimes appear, as do Glossy Black Cockatoos and Dusky Woodswallows. In the ferny rainforest, Australian Logrunners are abundant. Yellow-tailed Black Cockatoos are always a delight – they are both common and easily seen (and heard).

Fan-tailed Cuckoos are common and widespread. They are the only resident cuckoo here. While they generally prefer tall forests, their distinctive descending trill can be heard throughout the park. They always choose hosts much smaller than themselves, usually birds that build domed nests close to the ground, such as Rockwarblers, scrubwrens, heathwrens, fairywrens and thornbills. It's always very touching to see tiny little birds wearing themselves ragged feeding a much larger fat cuckoo fledgling. No wonder Fan-tailed Cuckoos live in the park: they have plenty of choice for hosts. As well as Rockwarblers and Chestnut-rumped

A Great Egret feeds happily at Fig Tree Flat in Royal National Park.

Heathwrens, there are three species of scrubwren (the most common being White-browed, but also reasonably common are Yellow-throated and Large-billed), two common fairywrens (Superb and Variegated) and two common thornbills (Brown and Striated).

Pacific Bazas are seen here in summer. They frequent the tall open forests and feed on stick insects. Black-faced Monarchs are common in summer around the rainforest, while Rose Robins come in winter and are best seen on the forest margins.

Seabirds can be seen from the cliff tops along the Coast Walk. Australasian Gannets can be seen plunge-diving into the sea. Little Penguins can sometimes be seen swimming, or heard yapping. Fluttering Shearwaters are common, mainly between July and November. White-bellied Sea Eagles can be seen at any time. The best time for albatross is winter and early spring when there are onshore winds. The most common species are Black-browed and Indian Yellow-nosed.

It's easy for birders to understand why Royal is Australia's most visited national park.

One of my very favourite birds, the Silvereye, is abundant throughout Royal National Park.

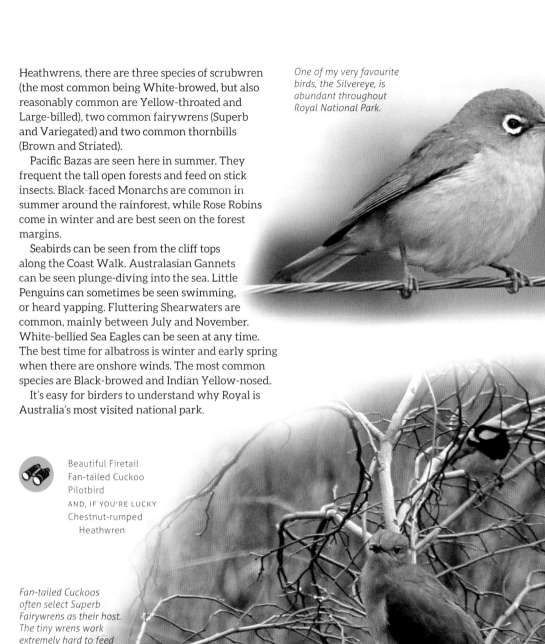

Beautiful Firetail
Fan-tailed Cuckoo
Pilotbird
AND, IF YOU'RE LUCKY
Chestnut-rumped
    Heathwren

Fan-tailed Cuckoos often select Superb Fairywrens as their host. The tiny wrens work extremely hard to feed the huge interloper.

87

Winton Wetlands

The female Australian Painted-snipe is more colourful than the male. This means that the male does all the egg sitting and chick rearing.

Winton Wetlands has a most impressive bird list and if I had witnessed a few of its very special sightings, there's no doubt it would be higher on my list of 100 sites than number 87. I'm thinking of birds such as Regent Honeyeaters, Australian Painted-snipe, Grey-crowned Babblers, Freckled Duck, Brolga and Lewin's Rail. All beautiful birds seen at Winton Wetlands, but, unfortunately, not by me.

Winton Wetlands, in north-east Victoria on the Hume Highway between Benalla and Wangaratta, comprises 3,000 hectares of swamp surrounded by red gum and box grassy woodlands. That's why the bird list is so extensive – the habitat accommodates lots of exciting bush birds together with wetland rarities.

This area was originally a series of smaller swamps. In 1970 it was turned into an irrigation reservoir known as Lake Mokoan, but it suffered from excessive evaporation and unhealthy blue-green algae. So the lake was decommissioned in

2010 and thus began Australia's largest wetland restoration project.

When you are travelling north on the Hume, there's a roadside stop which overlooks the wetlands and gives some idea of how vast they are. A map shows how to get to the other side where you

Winton Wetlands is a large swamp with a correspondingly large bird list.

| 184 |

can start birding. With very little effort, it's possible to see well over 70 species. And, who knows, you might just see a Southern Whiteface or a White-bellied Cuckooshrike. You might even see a Glossy Ibis or a Black-chinned Honeyeater.

It's exhilarating to know that you have a chance of seeing a Black Falcon or a critically endangered Swift Parrot, but it's even better to know that you're more than likely to see Diamond Firetails and Australasian Shovelers. You might possibly see a White-backed Swallow or a Zebra Finch or an Australian Crake, but you will probably see a Golden-headed Cisticola, a Brown Treecreeper and a Restless Flycatcher. Of course, you expect to see all the common waterbirds – ducks and swans, coots and ibis, herons and grebes – and all the common bush birds – Crested Pigeons, Peaceful Doves, Red-rumped Parrots and White-browed Babblers. There are raucous cockies and corellas and kookaburras, together with sweet little Superb Fairywrens, Striated Pardalotes and Crested Shriketits. My favourite bird, the Willie Wagtail, will probably greet you in the car park and Brown Falcons will sit quietly in a dead tree surveying the landscape.

In summer, Rainbow Bee-eaters add a touch of glamour, and Rufous Songlarks provide a musical accompaniment. If the eucalypts are flowering, look for Blue-faced Honeyeaters and if the mistletoe is flowering, watch out for gorgeous little Mistletoebirds. Check out the martins because there are both Tree and Fairy on the list and watch for Swamp Harriers flying over the wetlands, terrifying all the small birds on the water.

While Winton Wetlands boasts an extraordinary number of rare birds, its bird list is so comprehensive that even if you don't score a rarity, you're unlikely to come away disappointed.

You will probably see a Brown Treecreeper at Winton Wetlands. This is a female.

Brown Treecreeper
Horsfield's Bush Lark
Grey-crowned Babbler
AND, IF YOU'RE VERY LUCKY
Australian Painted-snipe
(summer)

88

Sacred Kingfishers often draw attention to themselves with their constant calling.

Sale Common State Game Refuge

Swamps are great places for crakes, rails, bitterns and snipe. Of course, there are also ducks, swans, pelicans and cormorants. And herons and gallinules.

Sale Common State Game Refuge is 300 hectares, of which 70 per cent is swamp. The rest is river red gum woodland and grassland. Sale is 260 kilometres east of Melbourne at the junction of the Princes and South Gippsland Highways. The common is adjacent to the South Gippsland Highway, where signs direct you to the entrance in a side street.

There is a boardwalk through the swamp, two bird hides, and an attractive walking track through red gum woodlands and grasslands. One deep waterhole ensures that there is always some water at Sale Common, when most of the swamp dries out during periods of drought. Once when I visited, eagerly anticipating some interesting wetland birds, I discovered there was no swamp – the ground was parched and cracked like an uninviting wasteland. On another occasion, when I was looking forward to a quiet saunter along the boardwalk, I arrived to find that there had been severe flood damage and the boardwalk was closed. Happily, at other times, I have enjoyed good birding at Sale Common.

I've watched gorgeous Golden-headed Cisticolas

Sale Common State Game Refuge has both bush birds and waterbirds.

perch on top of the reeds and sing with gusto. Little Grassbirds like to stay hidden and taunt birdwatchers with their three-note mournful call. Australian Reed Warblers (formerly and most appropriately called 'clamorous') chatter noisily from the reeds. Superb Fairywrens and Red-browed Finches share the boardwalk with birders and Australian Golden Whistlers call from the gum trees.

The grasslands are home to both Brown and Stubble Quail, and pardalotes and Mistletoebirds flit in and out of the trees. Both Sacred and Azure Kingfishers are on the bird list, as are both Australasian and Black-backed Bitterns.

The birds you are most likely to see are Superb Fairywrens, Straw-necked Ibis and Black Swans. You'll probably also see Whistling Kites, White-faced Herons and Australasian Swamphens. And I don't think I've been to Sale Common without seeing Brown Thornbills, Grey Fantails and Australian Golden Whistlers. But (who knows?) you might luck onto a Pink-eared Duck or a Glossy Ibis or a Red-necked Avocet.

As well as birds there are frogs and lizards, and I can confirm that there are snakes: copperheads, red-bellied blacks and tigers. Notwithstanding these reptiles, Sale Common is definitely worth a visit.

And while you're in Sale, take the opportunity to check out Lake Guyatt for Freckled Duck.

Australian Reed Warbler
Little Grassbird
Sacred Kingfisher
Australian Golden Whistler

Australian Reed Warblers are nondescript little birds with a very big voice.

Bronzewing Flora and Fauna Reserve

89

Dusky Woodswallows like open forest, so, while they are on the Bronzewing bird list, they are not common here.

Bronzewing Flora and Fauna Reserve must be one of Victoria's best kept birdy secrets. It is absent from many maps. There are no signs or obvious entry points. It is located on the Sunraysia Highway south of Ouyen. (Ouyen is 441 kilometres north-west of Melbourne and 100 kilometres south of Mildura.) The reserve comprises sandhills vegetated with low mallee eucalypts. The track is sandy and can be steep. A 4WD is essential.

It is a very special place for me, as it's where I saw my first Black-eared Miner. The entire Bronzewing population of Black-eared Miners is believed to have been destroyed in the dreadful 2014 fire which impacted the whole reserve. The total population of Black-eared Miners is about 500 birds, found mainly in Riverland Biosphere Reserve in South Australia.

The most common bird in Bronzewing Flora and Fauna Reserve is the Australian Magpie, followed by the Willie Wagtail, the Weebill and the White-winged Chough. Apart from swallows and martins, only three Australian birds construct their nests out of mud: Magpie-larks, Apostlebirds and White-winged Choughs. The nest in the photo belongs to a family of choughs.

Common Bronzewings live up to their name here and Chestnut Quail-thrush and Malleefowl are common too. What a treat! You will often come across a pair of Quail-thrush quietly going about their business, walking amongst the leaf litter, not disturbing anyone.

Malleefowl are usually alone and they have a stately march, as if they had all the time in the world, which, I guess, they have.

Mulga Parrots are the most common parrots, followed closely by Mallee Ringnecks. You can also see Eastern Bluebonnets. What you notice as they fly overhead is not their deep blue faces, but their bright red bellies.

In this dry country, Grey Currawongs are more common than the Pied one more familiar to city dwellers. The local race of Grey Currawongs are called Black-winged Currawongs. White-browed Woodswallows are seen more often than their Dusky cousins, while Jacky Winters waggle their tails and Grey Butcherbirds sing melodiously.

Splendid Fairywrens add a touch of colour, as do Spotted Pardalotes. If you're very lucky, you might see a Regent Parrot or a Southern Scrub Robin or even a Black Falcon.

It's a large reserve and an easy place in which to forget the urgency of city living and, like the Malleefowl, slow down to a stately pace.

White-winged Choughs are common at Bronzewing Flora and Fauna Reserve. One of their mud nests can be seen in the eucalypt.

Mulga Parrots like mallee scrub, so they're right at home at Bronzewing.

Malleefowl
Chestnut Quail-thrush
Spotted Pardalote
  (race *xanthopyge*)
Mulga Parrot

90

Rottnest Island

Quokkas and king skinks, beaches and bicycles – that about sums up Rottnest Island, south of Perth in Western Australia. It is a very pleasant place to spend a summer's day birding, and there's always a chance of a Red-necked Phalarope, a Little Ringed Plover or a Long-toed Stint.

You can get to Rottnest by ferry, either from Perth or from Fremantle. I remember seeing Brown Skuas from the ferry. You'll probably also see Australasian Gannets and Osprey that nest on the island. You might see shearwaters (Wedge-tailed or maybe Little if you're lucky) or an Indian Yellow-nosed Albatross in winter. In summer you might also see Bridled, Roseate or Fairy Terns. You will certainly see Silver Gulls, and Greater Crested and Caspian Terns.

Rottnest has bush birds, waterbirds and waders. Twitchers come here to tick introduced Indian Peafowl and Common Pheasant. Sometimes they pretend they're really looking for Rock Parrots or Banded Stilts or Banded Lapwings.

Australian Shelducks are abundant on Rottnest; Pacific Black Duck and Grey Teal are common. You'll certainly see pelicans, and Pied and Little Pied Cormorants. You can admire Red-capped Plovers as Nankeen Kestrels hover overhead. There's a good

Brown Skuas can be seen from the ferry to Rottnest Island.

Ospreys on Rottnest Island enjoy a view of Perth.

chance of Grey Plovers too. Red-necked Avocets breed on Rottnest and both Pied Stilts and Pied Oystercatchers are just about guaranteed. Pacific Reef Herons stalk along the rocky shoreline and White-fronted Chats play among the vegetation.

Sadly, the only pigeons on Rottnest are introduced: there are both Spotted and Laughing Doves. The Western Australian authorities, who are doing such a good job keeping out starlings, blackbirds, sparrows and mynas, seem to have accepted these doves willingly.

Galahs are abundant – full of character and very entertaining. I don't think you could call Australian Ravens entertaining, but they are present in good numbers. Willie Wagtails are definitely entertaining, cheerful and diverting. You'll have no trouble seeing Silvereyes or Spotted Scrubwren or Western Gerygones. You'll hear – and see – Singing Honeyeaters throughout the island.

Some of our most beautiful and most colourful birds are common on Rottnest. Birds like Rainbow Bee-eaters, Red-capped Robins and Sacred Kingfishers. And then there are Western Whistlers. Most male birds are satisfied with being either handsome or a good singer (or a good dancer). Western Whistlers are prodigal: they have both looks and voice.

Lots of captivating birds are easily seen on Rottnest and there's always a chance of some rarities. It's very good birding and so close to the capital city.

Osprey
Western Whistler
Rock Parrot
AND, IF YOU'RE LUCKY
Red-necked Phalarope (summer)

Western Whistlers are doubly blessed: they have both good looks and singing prowess.

91

Dusky Robins sit quietly and can sometimes be overlooked.

Mount Field National Park

Mount Field National Park has much to offer birders. Here you can see 11 out of the 12 Tasmanian endemics, missing out only on Forty-spotted Pardalotes. You are bound to see Tasmanian Nativehens, Green Rosellas, Yellow Wattlebirds, Tasmanian Scrubwrens, Tasmanian Thornbills and Black Currawongs; they are all very common. With a little effort, you should manage the three other honeyeaters (Yellow-throated, Black-headed and Strong-billed) and the pretty little Dusky Robin too. This is also a great place for other sought-after species like Crescent Honeyeaters, Pink Robins and Beautiful Firetails. In the wet forest you may see shy BassianThrush or hear the musical call of the Olive Whistler.

Mount Field is 75 kilometres, or just over an hour's drive, from Hobart. Park entry fees apply. Tasmania's first nature reserve was created around Mount Field in 1885 and in 1916 Mount Field was one of the first national parks to be proclaimed in Tasmania.

The park boasts several picturesque lakes, rivers and waterfalls and accommodates a variety of habitats: rainforests, fern forests, tall swamp gum forests and stunted snow gums in alpine terrain. You can see Tasmania's endemic celery-top pine, native laurels and perhaps most notably, the endemic golden Tasmanian deciduous beech, fagus. Perhaps it might be worth timing your visit for autumn, when it is a blaze of colour. On the other hand, in summer, the boronias, heath and waratahs are flowering. Weather can be unpredictable at any time of year and vehicles may require chains. I was there in October and there was plenty of snow around on the drive up to Lake Fenton. It is probably a good idea to call in at the visitors centre when you arrive. You can pick up some maps and assess the conditions of the day.

There are many walks in the park, ranging from a 15-minute stroll to overnight hikes. In my short visit, I managed to fit in three short walks: the Tall Trees Walk, the walk to Lady Barron Falls and the Lyrebird Nature Walk. This latter walk sounds fine until you realise that there is nothing natural about lyrebirds in Tasmania.

Some misguided conservationist introduced Superb Lyrebirds into Mount Field in 1934. The

Tasmanian Scrubwren
Tasmanian Nativehen
Tasmanian Thornbill
Green Rosella (race *caledonicus*)

While not endemic to Tasmania, Beautiful Firetails are more easily seen here.

intention was to prevent extinction of the birds on the mainland due to predation by foxes and hunting. Lyrebird numbers have exploded in Tasmania and, while there is no denying this is a very spectacular bird, it does not belong on this island state, scratching up the forest floor, disturbing plants and invertebrates that have evolved to survive without interference from such enormous feet.

However, there is nothing unnatural about the Yellow-tailed Black Cockatoos as they wail overhead. It is always uplifting to see these magnificent birds with their deep slow wing-beats.

The park was named after Barron Field, a judge who presided over the first sitting of Van Diemen's Land Supreme Court in 1819. In the same year, Barron Field published the first (albeit slim) volume of poetry in Australia. How apt to have such epic landscape named after Australia's first published poet!

Mount Field National Park is home to 11 out of the 12 Tasmanian endemics.

92

Mogareeka Inlet

The mouth of the Bega River on the Sapphire Coast of southern New South Wales is known as Mogareeka Inlet. It is situated five kilometres north of Tathra, five hours south of Sydney on the Princes Highway, or two and a half hours south-west of Canberra on the Snowy Mountains Highway. The Bega River mouth is closed to the sea more often than it is open, providing much local controversy about whether or not it should be dredged.

Mogareeka Inlet is a pleasant place to look for waders, bush birds and waterbirds.

Perhaps the most exciting species seen here is the Beach Stone-curlew – a grotesque-looking bird. Surely not even his mother could call him handsome. This must be the southern limit of his normal range (although vagrants have turned up in Victoria recently).

It is also the southern limit for Topknot Pigeons, Brown Cuckoo-doves and Yellow-throated Scrubwren. (Yes, I know that Topknot Pigeons have been seen as far south as Tasmania, but these are accidental sightings, not the bird's normal range.)

A colony of Little Terns breeds at Mogareeka Inlet each summer, although breeding success varies from year to year. Silver Gulls are a threat to the colony, taking both eggs and chicks if given half a chance. Occasionally, one pair of Fairy Terns is reported among the colony of Little Terns.

The mouth of the Bega River is known as Mogareeka Inlet and is a great spot for waders.

Caspian and Greater Crested Terns are common here too.

Hooded Plovers also breed here. They are officially classified as vulnerable, so every breeding success is a cause for celebration.

You may well see majestic White-bellied Sea Eagles flying overhead and elegant Great Egrets fishing in the shallows. In summer, Common Sandpipers and Far Eastern Curlews fly in for a visit, and you can see Pied and Sooty Oystercatchers at any time of year.

Around the brackish waters on the inland side of the highway, there are crakes and rails and Australasian Bitterns.

There are good bush birds here too: honeyeaters, lorikeets, Galahs and Superb Fairywrens, although on one occasion when I visited, there was an invasion of vociferous Bell Miners. The incessant tintinnabulation was ear-piercing. They are very pretty birds, with a very pretty little tinkle, but they do tend to dominate rather egotistically.

There are sometimes White-headed Pigeons sitting on the wires. Today, our warmer climate has encouraged Australasian Figbirds to venture this far south, as well as Pacific Koels and Channel-billed Cuckoos.

Altogether, quite an interesting bird list. But the chance of seeing a Beach Stone-curlew alone would be enough to persuade me to stop at Mogareeka Inlet.

Beach Stone-curlew
Little Tern
Topknot Pigeon
AND, IF YOU'RE LUCKY
Australasian Bittern

It is always exciting to see a Beach Stone-curlew. Surely this bird was created by a committee?

93 Booderee National Park

Apart from the many inviting beaches and coves, there are two spots I particularly like to go birding in Booderee National Park. One is the Botanic Gardens; the other is Telegraph Creek Nature Trail.

Booderee National Park is on Jervis Bay on the south coast of New South Wales, between Nowra and Ulladulla. It's about three hours' drive from either Sydney or Canberra. Entry fees apply. Eastern Bristlebirds are often seen on roadside verges in the park, hopping about happily, always a good bird to add to your day list.

The Booderee Botanic Gardens are the only Aboriginal-owned botanic gardens in Australia. They comprise 80 hectares of formal gardens, with paths and boardwalks meandering among them. There are picnic tables and toilet facilities. The gardens are fenced to keep wallabies out, but last time I was there I saw several kangaroos inside the fence, helpfully mowing the lawns to save the gardeners the effort.

There's always something of interest here. I've seen Satin Bowerbirds, Eastern Spinebills and Variegated Fairywrens. There are Eastern Whipbirds and Eastern Yellow Robins in the wet ferny gullies, and ducks and cormorants on the lake. I saw an Australasian Grebe here once. Honeyeaters abound in the flowering trees and shrubs. There are Lewin's, Yellow-faced, New Holland, Noisy Friarbirds, and both Red and Little Wattlebirds. I've

seen Olive-backed Orioles and Leaden Flycatchers, Australian Golden Whistlers and Varied Sittellas. Little wonder I enjoy birding here.

A few kilometres away, there are also picnic tables and a large car park, where Roger always waited patiently while I walked the Telegraph Creek Nature Trail. I live in hope of seeing an Eastern Ground Parrot here. The signage assures me that they are present, and who am I to doubt a notice that someone has taken the trouble to design, construct and erect? Perhaps the same official is responsible for the bench seat where you can sit watching the grassland, waiting for Eastern Ground Parrots to appear. I've seen Whistling Kites, Wedge-tailed Eagles and White-bellied Sea Eagles. And there are plenty of Eastern Bristlebirds here too.

Whether or not I ever tick Eastern Ground Parrots on this nature trail, it is a very pleasant, very easy short walk. There are Silvereyes and White-browed Scrubwrens. In summer, New Holland Honeyeaters predominate. In autumn, they're outnumbered by confusingly similar White-cheeked Honeyeaters and their Yellow-faced friends. There are Spotted Pardalotes and Southern Emu-wren.

'Booderee' means 'plenty of fish' in the local Aboriginal language. It might equally have been called 'plenty of birds'.

Yellow-faced Honeyeaters are migratory, but I often see them at Booderee.

Variegated Fairywrens have very long tails.

Murray's Track at Booderee National Park is a good place to see Eastern Bristlebirds.

Eastern Bristlebird
Eastern Whipbird
Variegated Fairywren
AND, IF YOU'RE VERY LUCKY
Eastern Ground Parrot

Yellow-tailed Black Cockatoos are easily identified by their wail and their slow wingbeat.

Kangaroo Island

94

I went to Kangaroo Island to see White-bellied Whipbirds (which I did easily) and the local race of Glossy Black Cockatoos (which I heard but did not see). This could be explained by the fact that, at the time, there were 2,000 whipbirds, but only 240 glossy blacks. This was before the devastating bushfires of 2019, which killed many birds and destroyed feeding habitat. Today it is estimated that there are just 1,000 whipbirds and 250 glossy blacks, whose population is increasing thanks to effective management.

Kangaroo Island, comprising 4,500 square kilometres, is Australia's third largest island. It is located at the entrance to St Vincent's Gulf in South Australia. The island has 509 kilometres of coastline, including rugged cliffs and pristine white beaches. The population is 4,400. More than a third of the island is protected in a National or Conservation Park. As there are no foxes or rabbits, the island teems with wildlife – wallabies, koalas, echidnas, platypus, goannas, seals, sea lions and, of course, kangaroos. There are wetlands, dense forest, coastal heath, mallee and sugar gum woodlands. No wonder the bird list comprises 267 species.

You can fly to Kangaroo Island, but we took the ferry from Cape Jervis on the tip of the Fleurieu Peninsula, 108 kilometres south of Adelaide. The ferry takes 45 minutes and I had hoped to see jaegers and skuas along the way. We were blessed with a smooth crossing, but no seabirds.

The observant birder will notice several endemic races on Kangaroo Island. The Red Wattlebirds are larger than their mainland cousins, and the Bush Stone-curlews are smaller. There are slight differences in plumage in Grey Currawongs and New Holland, Purple-gaped and Brown-headed Honeyeaters. The Silvereyes and Brown Thornbills are different too, but the variations are very subtle. Both Bassian Thrush and Crescent Honeyeaters are different from most of their mainland relations, but these races are not endemic to Kangaroo Island and spill over into the Mount Lofty Ranges.

Flinders Chase National Park comprises 33,000 hectares on the western end of the island. This is where you'll find the iconic Admirals Arch, and Remarkable Rocks, where the whipbirds are seen easily. This is one of few places where Brown-headed Honeyeaters are more common than New Hollands. There are lots of good birds here: Hooded Plovers, Sooty Oystercatchers, Yellow-tailed Black Cockatoos, Southern Emu-wrens, Tawny-crowned Honeyeaters and Beautiful Firetails, to name but a few.

We heard glossy blacks at Lathami Conservation Park, where nest boxes have been erected for them. One box had been commandeered by opportunistic Galahs when we were there. Today, nests are protected from invasion by possums and European honey bees, and ongoing management is required if breeding success is to be maintained.

The Brown-headed Honeyeaters on Kangaroo Island have a longer bill.

Murray Lagoon is in the north of Cape Gantheaume Conservation Park and is home to the island's largest freshwater lagoon. The bird list is enticing, but the lagoon was closed when we were on the island.

Cape Barren Geese were introduced in the 1930s and they certainly look quite at home now.

The baby seals are most endearing, the orchids are quite stunning, but for me, the White-bellied Whipbirds were the highlight of my trip to Kangaroo Island.

The White-bellied Whipbird is notoriously difficult to see, but I found them very easy on Kangaroo Island.

White-bellied Whipbird
Glossy Black Cockatoo
  (race *halmaturinus*)
Red Wattlebird (race
  clelandi)
Grey Currawong (race
  halmaturina)

Greater Crested Terns and
Silver Gulls loaf on the beach
at King Island.

95

King Island

My notes tell me that my one and only trip to King Island was wet and depressing. My memory is another thing altogether. I remember being delighted at seeing Scrubtits, which are classified as critically endangered on King Island. I remember a huge flock of White-throated Needletails (no doubt explained by the storms) and an hilarious agricultural show where locals competed in gumboot tossing.

King Island, which has an area of 1,100 square kilometres and a population of 1,700, is located in Bass Strait off the north-west tip of Tasmania, about halfway between Tasmania and the mainland.

Because of this location, it provides an ideal stopover for Orange-bellied Parrots on their annual migration from the mainland to nest in southern Tasmania. Orange-bellied Parrots are critically endangered: the population is estimated at 25 birds. Accordingly, King Island has been declared an Important Bird Area by BirdLife International.

Wild Turkey
Common Pheasant
Green Rosella (race *brownii*)
Black Currawong (race *colei*)

The Black Currawongs
are a different race on
King Island.

Liz Stimson

BirdLife International also acknowledges the presence of Hooded Plovers, a large colony of Short-tailed Shearwaters, other nesting seabirds (namely Fairy Terns, Pacific Gulls, Black-faced Cormorants, and both Sooty and Pied Oystercatchers), Flame Robins, and several endemic subspecies of bush bird.

There are no Tasmanian Nativehens on King Island, nor are there any Forty-spotted Pardalotes. You can see all the other Tasmanian endemics here (but bear in mind that Scrubtits are critically endangered and may be hard to find). Masked Lapwings, never rare in the right habitat within their range, are particularly common on King Island (and throughout Tasmania, for that matter). Cape Barren Geese are seen frequently, and Black Swans, Australian Magpies, Welcome Swallows and Silvereyes are abundant.

Serious twitchers go to King Island to add Wild Turkey and Common Pheasant to their lifelists. Such introduced birds are called 'plastic' ticks and, while twitchers affect contempt for non-natives, you'll note that such birds always manage somehow to appear on their lists. (Other introduced birds on King Island are Indian Peafowl, California Quail, Mallard, Eurasian Skylark, European Goldfinch and European Greenfinch as well as the inevitable starlings, blackbirds and House Sparrows.)

Obsessive twitchers go to King Island to see the endangered local race of Black Currawong, which may be slightly smaller, but otherwise looks exactly the same as his slightly larger Tasmanian cousin. These same compulsive twitchers will be pleased to see vulnerable King Island Green Rosellas, which are the same size as their Tasmanian relations and look precisely the same. Who can fathom the mind of the driven twitcher?

King Island does not leap to mind as a top Australian birding site, and has only gained recent prominence with the decline of the Orange-bellied Parrot. Twitchers, intent on getting their plastic ticks, can now dress up their journey as a respectable quest for a critically endangered parrot.

King Island also has its own race of Green Rosellas.

96

Ikara-Flinders Ranges National Park

The Flinders Ranges are better known for spectacular scenery than for great birdwatching. When I think of the Flinders Ranges, I think of dry creekbeds lined with ancient river red gums, dramatic rugged mountain ranges and half a dozen euros peering inquisitively through the morning mist over a hillside covered with spinifex. But there are good birds here too. Red-capped Robins and Mallee Ringnecks are common. Galahs are so abundant we take them for granted. A soaring Wedge-tailed Eagle is a breathtaking sight no matter how often you see it. Of course, there are always Emus, Australian Magpies and Australian Ravens. In fact, there are 146 species on the list.

Red-backed Kingfishers prefer hot, dry country, so they quite enjoy the Flinders Ranges.

The national park is in the northern Flinders Ranges, between Hawker and Blinman, 450 kilometres north of Adelaide. The park comprises 912 square kilometres of picturesque South Australian outback.

Without a doubt the most sought-after bird in the Ikara-Flinders Ranges National Park is the Short-tailed Grasswren, always difficult to see – as I can attest. I will not admit here how many hours I have wasted trying to see this little bird. Suffice it to say that, had I spent

Ikara-Flinders Ranges National Park is home to 146 bird species.

this time productively, I might have replicated the Bayeux tapestry or qualified as a jet pilot. I finally managed to see my Short-tailed Grasswren (with professional help) in 2013.

The most common honeyeaters are Yellow-throated Miners and handsome Spiny-cheeked Honeyeaters with their distinctive friendly call. Less common are Singing, White-plumed, subtly understated Brown-headed and prized Grey-fronted.

Black Kites are often seen patrolling the roads in the early morning searching for some unlucky creature killed in the night. Red-backed Kingfishers sit quietly in the gum trees, often overlooked until they fly.

Elegant Parrots, so aptly named, flash past in a rush or walk unobtrusively on the ground. There are Purple-backed and striking White-winged Fairywrens, darling small Southern Whiteface and pretty Redthroats.

Pigeons are represented by Common Bronzewings, endearing Peaceful Doves and comical, now almost ubiquitous, Crested Pigeons. Give any bird a crest and it turns into a veritable clown. Crested Pigeons are full of character and their footprints make most

The sought-after Grey-fronted Honeyeater can be found in the Flinders Ranges.

artistic patterns in the sand.

White-browed Babblers are clowns too. They are often seen in the park and their Chestnut-crowned cousins are sometimes seen too.

You can hear Weebills make their disproportionately loud call for such a tiny bird (indeed this is Australia's smallest bird) and Striated Pardalotes are vocal throughout the park.

The Flinders Ranges has many special birds, and birdwatchers will not be disappointed, unless, like me, all they want to see is a Short-tailed Grasswren. Or maybe they will be successful in this – with or without professional assistance.

Grey-fronted Honeyeater
Redthroat
Elegant Parrot
AND, IF YOU'RE VERY LUCKY
Short-tailed Grasswren

Clem Walton Park, Cloncurry

97

Great Crested Grebes are buffoons. It is always a thrill to see them.

Clem Walton Park, north of Cloncurry in far north-west Queensland, is a very pretty spot. I've only been here once, but I would gladly come again. The birds were wonderful. Among other things, I remember counting 34 Caspian Terns along with nine Great Crested Grebes at one large dam. To see a single Caspian Tern or Great Crested Grebe is always good – birders don't expect to see either of these species in flocks.

We started the day in Cloncurry, entertained by the raucous rasping and hissing from a multitude of Spotted Bowerbirds. Then we admired Cloncurry Parrots, which are a smaller, paler race of Australian Ringnecks with yellow underparts, a green head and no red frontal band. The locals call them 'buln buln'. We stopped again for Pictorella Mannikins at a soak in Slaty Creek, where they were joined by budgies, doves and other finches.

Cloncurry Parrot (aka Australian
    Ringneck, race *macgillivrayi*)
Caspian Tern
Great Crested Grebe
AND, IF YOU'RE VERY LUCKY
Kalkadoon Grasswren

Clem Walton Park on the Corella River in Cloncurry is an excellent spot and perhaps deserves to be higher than number 97 on my list.

Sue Taylor

We finally dragged ourselves away and set off for Clem Walton Park on the Corella River, some 60 kilometres west of Cloncurry. The sun was shining and the birds were singing. It was a perfect day.

There is a possibility of Kalkadoon Grasswren in the vicinity of the park and there is at least one local Pheasant Coucal. We didn't see either.

What we did see were waterbirds and bush birds – lots of them. We saw Brolga, Australian Pelicans, Australasian Darters and three sorts of cormorant (Great, Little Pied and Little Black). We saw Masked Lapwings, Pied Stilts, and Black-fronted and Red-kneed Dotterels. We were here in July, so we didn't expect any summer migrants. There were moorhen and ducks (Grey Teal, Pacific Black Duck and Hardhead) and Australasian as well as the aforementioned Great Crested Grebes.

A Red-winged Parrot added a flash of colour and a Whistling Kite whistled his recognisable call, seemingly so inappropriate for a raptor. A Sacred Kingfisher sat quietly in a gum tree and a friendly Willie Wagtail chattered around our feet. Grey-crowned Babblers made their presence felt too, whistling and babbling with excitement.

In the southern states, we only see Rufous Songlarks in the summer; in winter, at least some of them migrate to Clem Walton Park.

A Cuckooshrike invited much debate as to its identity: was it our familiar black-faced friend, or was it his white-bellied cousin? Better looks confirmed it was our well-known companion, known to birders as 'Bufcus', an attempted rendition of its abbreviated name, BFCS.

This photo shows why some people call Australasian Darters 'Snake Birds'.

Honeyeaters included Little Friarbirds, Spiny-cheeked, Singing and Yellow-tinted, and Woodswallows were represented by both Masked and White-browed.

The consensus was that Clem Walton Park was a great spot and I, for one, want to return to look for Kalkadoon Grasswren.

Royal Botanic Gardens Cranbourne

98

The 363-hectare site which makes up the Royal Botanic Gardens Cranbourne is about one-third native gardens and two-thirds untouched remnant bush. Cranbourne is 43 kilometres south-east of Melbourne. The gardens are on the corner of Ballarto Road and Botanic Drive, about 500 metres past the racecourse. Entry is free and the gardens are open from 9 am until 5 pm every day except Christmas Day and days of total fire ban. If you walk to Trig Point Lookout, you'll have great views of Melbourne, Mount Macedon, Western Port and Port Phillip Bay.

This is the place to go to see southern brown bandicoots. These cute little furry creatures are very common in the car park and around the cafe.

The Cranbourne bush comprises heathy woodlands and wetlands, and the bird list reflects these diverse habitats with waterbirds, bush birds and birds that like heathlands, such as Southern Emu-wren. You will certainly see New Holland Honeyeaters and Superb Fairywrens, Eastern Yellow Robins and Grey Fantails. I always hope for a Brush Bronzewing. All three grebes are featured on the bird list, along with Bassian Thrush and Black-tailed Nativehen. There are Blue-winged

Parrots, Masked Woodswallows and White-throated Treecreepers.

The Cranbourne bird list includes a surprising number of rare and threatened species. There are birds such as Black Falcon, Chestnut-rumped Heathwren, Australasian Bittern, Lewin's Rail and Freckled Duck. Which, of course, is not to say that you can go to Cranbourne and see a Black Falcon. Rather, someone once saw a Black Falcon here. Of course, anyone can hope to luck onto a rarity and it is reassuring to know that Glossy Ibis and Grey Goshawk have been recorded here.

Leaving aside these improbable treasures, what are you likely to see? The honeyeaters are usually cooperative, with White-plumed, White-eared, and White-naped all present along with Bell Miners and Red Wattlebirds. Sometimes there's an invasion of Yellow-faced Honeyeaters and sometimes Eastern Spinebill put in an appearance. You'll hear and see both Grey Shrikethrushes and

One of my favourite little birds, Superb Fairywrens, hop around your feet at the Royal Botanic Gardens Cranbourne.

New Holland Honeyeater
Eastern Spinebill
Grey Shrikethrush
Superb Fairywren

Straw-necked Ibis
may be common, but
their long downturned
bill makes them most
elegant.

The Royal Botanic Gardens
Cranbourne have remnant
bush as well as wetlands.

Spotted Pardalotes, and White-browed Scrubwren will certainly hop amongst the undergrowth. Don't forget the black-and-white brigade: Australian Magpies, Magpie-larks and Willie Wagtails. Welcome Swallows will definitely swoop overhead and Brown Thornbills will play in the foliage. Australasian Swamphen will strut their stuff near the water. Last time I was here, I saw a Straw-necked Ibis and a Brown Goshawk. And several southern brown bandicoots.

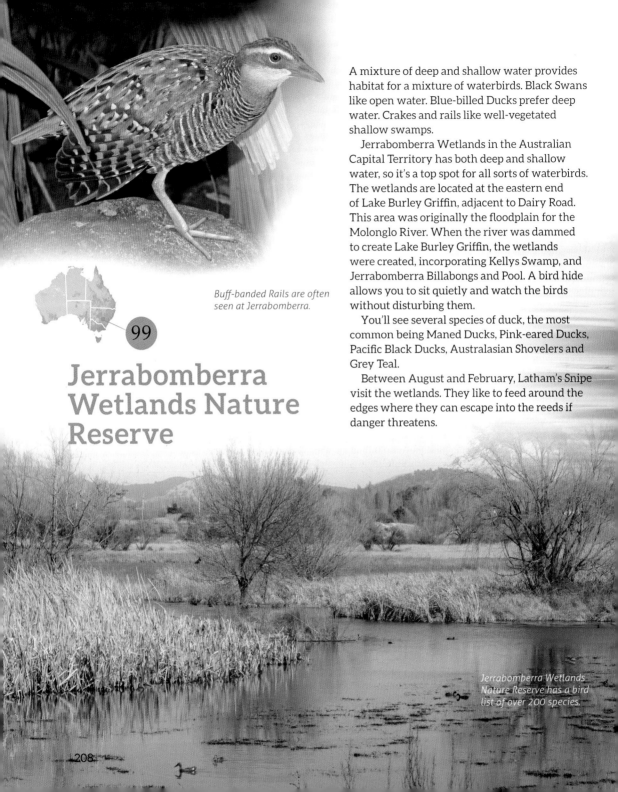

A mixture of deep and shallow water provides habitat for a mixture of waterbirds. Black Swans like open water. Blue-billed Ducks prefer deep water. Crakes and rails like well-vegetated shallow swamps.

Jerrabomberra Wetlands in the Australian Capital Territory has both deep and shallow water, so it's a top spot for all sorts of waterbirds. The wetlands are located at the eastern end of Lake Burley Griffin, adjacent to Dairy Road. This area was originally the floodplain for the Molonglo River. When the river was dammed to create Lake Burley Griffin, the wetlands were created, incorporating Kellys Swamp, and Jerrabomberra Billabongs and Pool. A bird hide allows you to sit quietly and watch the birds without disturbing them.

You'll see several species of duck, the most common being Maned Ducks, Pink-eared Ducks, Pacific Black Ducks, Australasian Shovelers and Grey Teal.

Between August and February, Latham's Snipe visit the wetlands. They like to feed around the edges where they can escape into the reeds if danger threatens.

Buff-banded Rails are often seen at Jerrabomberra.

99

Jerrabomberra Wetlands Nature Reserve

Jerrabomberra Wetlands Nature Reserve has a bird list of over 200 species.

This is also the place to look for crakes and rails. Buff-banded Rails are often seen; the rarer Lewin's Rail is here too. Baillon's, Spotless and Australian Crakes are all on the list. Another much sought-after species, the Australian Painted-snipe, also frequents these wetlands. These fascinating birds have sex role reversal: she's the more brightly coloured, he's smaller and duller. This means that he's the one who sits on the eggs. It's always the bird with more subdued colours that takes on the job of sitting quietly, hoping not to be noticed.

Golden-headed Cisticolas and Little Grassbirds. Superb Fairywrens and Silvereyes are both common, while Red Wattlebirds and Yellow-faced Honeyeaters frequent nearby bushes. There are Crested Pigeons, Galahs and Sulphur-crested Cockatoos. You'll see Rufous Whistlers and White-browed Scrubwren, Australian Magpies, Pied Currawongs and Magpie-larks.

Around 200 birds have been recorded here, so while Jerrabomberra Wetlands may be second last on my list, it is certainly well worth a visit.

As well as these titillating species, there are all the common waterbirds you'd expect at Jerrabomberra. There are cormorants, ibis and spoonbills, moorhens, swamphens and coots. There are Australasian Darters, Australian Pelicans, Australasian Grebes, White-faced Herons and Great Egrets. In summer, Sharp-tailed Sandpipers visit from Siberia. Pied Stilts can be seen all year round. There are Masked Lapwings, and Black-fronted and Red-kneed Dotterels.

In the reeds there are Australian Reed Warblers,

Australasian Shovelers are easily identified by their shovel-shaped bill.

Latham's Snipe (summer)
Australasian Shoveler
Red-browed Finch
Buff-banded Rail

100 Alice Springs sewage ponds

Local birders may be upset to see the Alice Springs sewage ponds last on my list. But let's face it, when you have 100 sites, one of them has to be number 100. On a recent trip, I set out to revisit these ponds, but soon heard that the plant was closed. So I returned home. Had I made it, and managed to see, say, a Grey Wagtail, or a Swinhoe's Snipe, there is no doubt that the Alice Springs sewage ponds would have rocketed up my list. As it is, I did not.

Australian Pipits are common at the Alice Springs sewage ponds.

The Alice Springs sewage ponds (otherwise known as the Alice Springs Waste Stabilisation Ponds or Ilparpa Ponds) are located six kilometres south of the town. You need permission and a key to enter the plant, which must be obtained from the Power and Water Corporation in town during office hours.

Having said that, with a bird list comprising 185 species, it is a special place, well deserving to be included in Australia's top birding sites.

Naturally the main attractions are waterbirds and waders, but there are other birds of interest too. Australian Pipits are very common and there's a good chance of a Zebra Finch. No matter how often I see these dear little birds, I have to pause and admire their beauty. I can't help anthropomorphizing and giving them all sweet personalities to match their engaging appearance.

Black Kites are a certainty and Whistling Kites more than likely. There are 16 raptors on the list, but the others are not seen very often. The next most likely one is the Nankeen Kestrel.

You will see a Little Crow and a Torresian Crow, but will you know the difference? The Little Crow is (appropriately) smaller, with longer legs and is most easily recognized by its nasal call: 'Nark, nark, nark'. The Torresian Crow shuffles its wings on landing.

You'll certainly see Magpie-larks and (my favourite) Willie Wagtails. You will see spectacular White-winged Fairywrens (how I wish we had them closer to home!) and comical Crested Pigeons. You will hear the three-note mournful call of the Little Grassbird, but they can be difficult to see. Unlike in the southern states, Australian Reed Warblers are present here all year round.

But, as I say, the main attractions are waterbirds and waders, and there are lots of them. There are ducks and swans, pelicans and grebes, cormorants and darters. There are ibis and spoonbills, herons and egrets. There are crakes, rails, swamphens, coots and nativehens.

And then there are the waders. Apart from the usual suspects (Black-fronted and Red-kneed Dotterels, Red-capped Plovers, Masked Lapwings), in summer you'll see not only Sharp-tailed Sandpiper, but also Wood and here, obligingly, the Common Sandpiper lives up to its name. Common Greenshanks do too, and Marsh Sandpipers and Australian Pratincoles are seen frequently.

And then there's what gets the twitchers twitching – the chance of a rarity. Little Curlews, Long-toed Stints and Red-necked Phalaropes have all been reported. Ruffs are much more likely than Eastern Yellow Wagtails, and Pectoral Sandpipers are seen more frequently than their Broad-billed cousins. But they're all on the list, so there's probably more chance of seeing them than of winning the lottery.

Black Kite
Australian Pratincole
Common Sandpiper (summer)
Little Crow

Red-capped Plovers are present all year round.

Bibliography

Anyon-Smith, W (2006) *Birdwatching in Royal & Heathcote National Parks*, NSW National Parks and Wildlife Service, Sydney.

Bransbury, J (1987) *Where to Find Birds in Australia*, Hutchinson, Melbourne.

Christidis, L & Boles, WE (2008) *Systematics and Taxonomy of Australian Birds*, CSIRO Publishing, Melbourne.

Garnett ST & Baker GB (Eds) (2021) *The Action Plan for Australian Birds 2020*, CSIRO Publishing, Melbourne.

Garnett, ST, Szabo, JK & Dutson, G (2010) *The Action Plan for Australian Birds 2010*, CSIRO Publishing, Melbourne.

Higgins, PJ et al. (1990–2006) *Handbook of Australian, New Zealand & Antarctic Birds*, Volumes 1–7, Oxford University Press, Melbourne.

Menkhorst, P, Rogers, D & Clarke, R (2017) *The Australian Bird Guide*, CSIRO Publishing, Melbourne.

Nielsen, L (1996) *Birds of Queensland's Wet Tropics and Great Barrier Reef*, Gerard Industries Proprietary Limited, Bowden, South Australia.

—— (2003) *Birding Australia: A Directory of Australian Birding*, Lloyd Nielsen, Mount Molloy, Queensland.

—— (2006) *Birding Australia Site Guide: The South-East*, Lloyd Nielsen, Mount Molloy, Queensland.

Onley, D & Scofield, P (2007) *Field Guide to the Albatrosses, Petrels and Shearwaters of the World*, Christopher Helm, London.

Pizzey, G & Knight F (1997) *Field Guide to the Birds of Australia*, Harper Collins, Sydney.

Simpson, K & Day, N (2010) *Field Guide to the Birds of Australia*, Viking, Camberwell, Victoria.

Thomas, R, Thomas, S, Andrew, D & McBride, A (2011) *The Complete Guide to Finding the Birds of Australia*, CSIRO Publishing, Melbourne.

Index

Sites by States and Territories

Numbers denote site numbers

AUSTRALIAN CAPITAL TERRITORY

Booderee National Park	93
Jerrabomberra	99

NEW SOUTH WALES

Ash Island	12
Barren Grounds Nature Reserve	46
Barrington Tops National Park	59
Capertee Valley	48
Comerong Island Nature Reserve	39
Cootamundra	84
Cowra	85
Fivebough Swamp, Leeton	64
Kiama Pelagic	10
Kinchega National Park	37
Ku-Ring-Gai Chase National Park	62
Lake Cargelligo sewage treatment works	68
Lord Howe Island	60
Mogareeka Inlet	92
Round Hill Nature Reserve	72
Royal National Park	86
Stockton Sandspit	38
Sturt National Park	66
The Rock Nature Reserve – Kengal Aboriginal Place	15
Wonga Wetlands	54

NORTHERN TERRITORY

Adelaide River Crossing	76
Alice Springs sewage ponds	100
Buffalo Creek	61
Darwin	11
Fogg Dam	25
Kakadu National Park	18
Katherine	80
Knuckey Lagoon	34
Tjoritja/West MacDonnell National Park	73

OTHER AUSTRALIAN TERRITORIES

Cocos (Keeling) Islands	7
Christmas Island	21
Norfolk Island	67

QUEENSLAND

Abattoir Swamp	81
Cairns	3
Cape York	36
Clem Walton Park, Cloncurry	97
Cumberland Dam	45
Daintree River cruise	24
Hasties Swamp	32
Julatten	8
Kutini-Payamu (Iron Range) National Park	27
Lake Bindegolly National Park	75
Lamington National Park	6
Mareeba Tropical Savanna and Wetland Reserve	33
Mission Beach	49
Rinyirru (Lakefield) National Park	77
Townsville Town Common Conservation Park	9

SOUTH AUSTRALIA

Birdsville Track	41
Bool Lagoon Game Reseve	70
Dhilba Guuranda-Innes National Park	69
Gluepot Reserve	26
Ikara-Flinders Ranges National Park	96
Kangaroo Island	94
Lake Gilles Conservation Park	52
Port Augusta	47
Strzlecki Track	56

This edition first published by John Beaufoy Publishing in the United Kingdom and Australia in 2023

11 Blenheim Court, 316 Woodstock Road, Oxford OX2 7NS, England

www.johnbeaufoy.com

Originally published as *Best 100 Birdwatching Sites in Australia* by NewSouth Publishing in 2013

10 9 8 7 6 5 4 3 2 1

ISBN 978-1-913679-51-4

2nd edition designed by Gulmohur
Original design by Di Quick

Project management by Rosemary Wilkinson

Printed and bound in Malaysia by Times Offset (M) Sdn. Bhd.